Letters to My Teacher

Tributes to the People
Who Have Made a Difference

Edited by
BARB KARG AND
RICK SUTHERLAND

Adams Media
Avon, Massachusetts

This book is dedicated to our extraordinary family members who continually touch our lives and our hearts: Ma, Pop, Dad, Dottie, Chris, Glen, Kathy, Anne, Terry Bob, and the Blonde Bombshell.
WE LOVE YOU ALL.

It is also a tribute to all our wonderful friends, and to the teachers, past and present, who have touched our lives. And to Sasha and Harley, two of our beloved felines, who passed on during the making of this book. Eternal thanks and love for being such amazing children.
You will always be with us.

Published by Adams Media, an F+W Publications Company
57 Littlefield Street
Avon, MA 02322
www.adamsmedia.com

Printed in Canada.
J I H G F E D C B

ISBN 10: 1-59337-603-0
ISBN 13: 978-1-59337-603-1
Library of Congress Cataloging-in-Publication Data
Letters to my teacher : tributes to the people who have made a difference /
edited by Barb Karg and Rick Sutherland.
p. cm.
ISBN 1-59337-603-0
1. Teachers. I. Karg, Barbara. II. Sutherland, Rick.
LB1775.L395 2006
371.1--dc22
2005033321

This publication is designed to provide accurate and authoritative information with regard to the subject matter covered. It is sold with the understanding that the publisher is not engaged in rendering legal, accounting, or other professional advice. If legal advice or other expert assistance is required, the services of a competent professional person should be sought.
—From a *Declaration of Principles* jointly adopted by a Committee of the American Bar Association and a Committee of Publishers and Associations

This book is available at quantity discounts for bulk purchases.
For information, please call 1-800-289-0963.

Acknowledgments

Many extraordinary individuals were involved in the making of *Letters to My Teacher*. As anyone who has worked on an anthology can attest, an amazing amount of love, patience, and tenacity is reflected on each page.

We have many fine folks to thank for helping us make this project a reality. From conception to writing to design and print—everyone did their part in no small measure, and for that, we are privileged to have worked with you.

To all of our contributors we offer a heartfelt salute. You are simply magnificent. Without a doubt, we know your letters will touch the hearts of your teachers, families, and everyone who has the honor of reading this book. Thank you for your hard work and above all, for your receptive warmth, humor, and the courage it took to share such personal experiences.

We'd also like to thank the wonderful folks at Adams Media, Inc for producing *Letters to My Teacher*. Endless gratitude to our dear friend Paula Munier, without whom this book wouldn't have come to fruition. You da' bomb, lady! Thanks also to Kate Epstein for her hard work and help in overseeing the process, and Meredith O'Hayre for her expert project management.

Thanks also go out to edit guru Laura Daly, copy chief Brett Palana-Shanahan, and copyeditor Sandra Smith for their keen editing eyes, and to Sue Beale and the design crew.

From the bottom of our hearts, we'd like to send out a special thank you to Trudi Karg, whose supreme organizational skills, editing, proofing, and motherly humor kept us humming from start to finish. What you did was amazing. We couldn't have done it without you, Ma!

Lastly, we'd like to thank all the teachers of the world who have taught us so many valuable life lessons. It's not often that you see the fruits of your labor, but with *Letters to My Teacher* it is our fondest hope that at long last you realize how much your teachings have impacted so many individuals.

Thank you all for making this such a wonderful experience and an exceptional book!

Barb Karg and Rick Sutherland
SEPTEMBER 2005

Contents

Introduction

Learning has always been part the human experience. Whether it be a caveman, computer whiz, butcher, baker, or candlestick maker, everyone learns from others. Observation and instinct are elements crucial to our very survival. We learn by listening, seeing, and doing, and what we lack in classical understanding, we make up for in innate awareness.

Teachers are masters of observation and intuition. With their keen eye and sonar hearing, they can sense even the slightest disturbance, emotional response, or potential action. Theirs is a world of infinite change and infinite possibility. As students and human beings, we possess certain common characteristics, but no two individuals are alike, and no situation or circumstance is identical to another. Teachers are the caretakers of intuition, and while the faces may change, the eternal thirst for knowledge and personal exploration remains strong.

For their efforts and abilities, teachers command respect. They don't always get that respect, but the very nature of their pursuit is as noble a cause as fighting for all that is good in this world. It's high time we let them know that their work and their very humanity is priceless to us, and that even the smallest of actions or absence of words has spoken volumes.

Having been raised in that prehistoric land before color television and microwave popcorn, we hold letters near and dear to our hearts. *Letters to My Teacher* has been a labor of love for us. As individuals who've learned much from the teachers we've had, we felt a burning desire to thank a group of stellar, hardworking professionals who rarely reap the benefit of their harvest after lovingly planting the seeds.

Rick's teacher Mrs. Howarth and Barb's professor Jack Hicks remain a constant source of inspiration, and their teachings played a large part in allowing us to bring this book to fruition. We owe both of them eternal thanks for instilling in us the drive and ambition to live our lives with dignity, class, and a rather large dose of humor.

This anthology is a testament to teachers around the globe. Reading these wonderful letters gives one a sense of place, time, occasion, and, above all, heartfelt thanks to those teachers who so greatly affected the lives of these students. Letters are written to teachers all over the world by former students ranging in age from three to eighty-five. Their experiences run the gamut from life fulfilling to live saving, and we hope they touch your hearts just as they have ours.

We all have strong influences in our lives. We observe and are observed, and our lives and the actions we take are a constant and infinite source of learning. Each of us is a teacher in our own right, but if not for the influential educators among us, we'd perhaps never even realize it.

To all of the amazing individuals who contributed to this collection, we say this: your enthusiasm, humor, intelligence, receptiveness, and grace are nothing short of astounding. Thank you for sharing your hearts and words with us and letting the world share in your personal triumphs. Your friends, family, colleagues, and especially your own teachers should be very proud.

To those of you who teach, let this anthology serve as thanks, honor, admiration, and high praise for the work you accomplish on a daily basis and throughout your career. Although you may not always see the direct effect your teachings have had on an individual, rest assured, you've made an impact. We may not always show you our thanks, but in writing to you, we honor you as educators and professionals, and above all, we cherish you as individuals.

The dog may have eaten our homework, but we have you to thank for the life lessons we retain and pass on to future generations.

From the bottom of our hearts, we thank you all.

Barb Karg and Rick Sutherland
AUGUST 1, 2005

1. You Are My Hero

What is it that makes a hero? Is it the fireman who pulls you from a burning building? Is it the parent who comforts you in your time of need? Is it an animal who provides you endless companionship? The very nature of a hero is indefinable and as unique as the individuals we are. Teachers are heroes who, whether they realize it or not, have saved us from ourselves and others at times when we needed them most. Their courage and foresight bestow upon us the greatest gift of all: freedom.

With their guidance, nurturing, and wisdom, we learn that not every piece of knowledge gained comes from a book. We learn that life itself is the ultimate teacher, and thankfully, we've found someone to point us in the right direction. We've felt the warmth and spirit that come from someone championing our cause and giving us the tools to make life an extraordinary journey.

There isn't a single individual on the planet who can honestly admit that he or she doesn't have a hero. Many of our heroes are teachers, who for better or worse allowed us to see with better eyes than our own. Everyone gets lost in clouds of doubt. Fear, hesitation, terror are the bogeymen hiding in our closets. Teachers open the door and let the light shine in. Whether spoken or not, their words and actions prove time and again that heroic efforts are inherent to their being, and for that they shall forever remain icons of battles worth fighting and worth winning.

Look, Listen, and Learn

By Megan McGregor

Dear Mrs. Johnson,

I have been a new student many times in my life, but never do I remember a time as well as when I started in your class in Melbourne, Australia. You taught me English in Year 10: poetry, writing, Shakespeare, genres—all my favorite things. You also taught speech writing and debating and public speaking—subjects that made me nauseous just thinking about them.

Growing up, I had always been an "in-betweener." Never popular enough for the "in" crowd, but never geeky or unlikable enough to belong to those groups that regularly got picked on or targeted by the popular kids. I was in the in-between group—the individuals that popular kids would consult if they needed help with homework, or if you were having a huge party, you invited them anyway; the ones you could say hello to in the hallways, even if you never would sit with them at lunch. We were the people who were not cool enough to be noticed, but not uncool enough to be noticed either—so we were generally ignored. But that's okay. That's how in-betweeners like it. After all, we have each other.

I started at the school and slipped into my usual pattern of being an in-betweener. I met good friends (all in-betweeners, of course), made good grades (not top grades, naturally), and was generally having fun.

3

That is, until second term started and you announced to us that we would be doing public speaking as a unit—including debating. That's when the trouble started.

In-betweeners are not built for public speaking. Public speaking involves being the center of attention and having everyone's eyes on *you*. I was in shock. I felt sick. I was going to cry. No, I wasn't . . . *that* would draw attention.

Over the next week during lunch, our group discussed the upcoming ordeal—about what we would do to avoid notice while being the center of attention. It wasn't too hard as time went on. By our account, all the pointers and tips we received as we worked through the theory of public speaking just had to be reversed: instead of learning to grab the audience's attention, we wanted to deflect it.

Imagine my surprise when I couldn't deflect! I always thought I would never be able to stand up in front of an audience, never be able to talk with everyone's eyes watching me; everyone looking at me, listening to me. But I was talking about something I cared about, and I couldn't do it: I couldn't bring myself to deflect everyone's attention from me and the issue—it was bigger than me, more important. I can't even remember the subject. It could have been about pollution or why the miniskirt should never make a comeback, but I do know that it was important to me at the time.

After a very shaky and nervous start, I found myself becoming more social. I was now trying to convince people with arguments, just by talking to them and giving them logical reasons. I was no longer looking for ways to get people to stop noticing me, instead looking for ways to convince them (well, at least when I had good a subject and some well-researched subject matter). I joined the debating team, and I think I shocked myself as much as I shocked my parents, but it felt good.

I want to say thank you, Mrs. Johnson, for introducing me to this. Who knows if I would have ever discovered this ability until it was too late. Thank you for saving me from being the wrong kind of in-betweener. Now, I am an in-betweener of the best kind—someone who knows when to be quiet and listen and when to argue a point or discuss an issue.

Your lessons serve me every day, because now I am a teacher myself, and I try to teach my students the same things you taught to me: Speak up, know what you're talking about, always make eye contact, and most importantly, always believe in yourself, because if you don't, why should anyone else?

Thank you.

BEST WISHES AND FOND REGARDS,
YOUR ONCE-UPON-A-TIME STUDENT,

Megan McGregor
Melbourne, Australia

Megan McGregor is a full-time teacher and part-time writer. Work and life have taken her from Australia to China and, most recently, to Northern Ireland.

Weak Feet

🍎 By Indi Zeleny 🍎

Dear Patsy,

I met you when I was six years old. I went to your
ballet class because my pediatrician told my mother
that I had weak feet. He said that ballet or swimming
would strengthen them, so Mom immediately enrolled
me in both. Overachievement, it seemed, was to run in
the family.

I stood before you and my little classmates in a
baggy leotard two sizes too big ("You'll grow into it,"
my mom assured me), barely able to turn out my feet,
point my toes, or kick a leg in the air without toppling
over. I was clumsy and shy.

You, on the other hand, were graceful and
petite, soft-spoken and kind, reassuring and gentle
in a motherly way that my mother was not. I'd been
apprehensive about this new class, this dance class. I
had heard of the ballet teachers who still carried sticks,
who spoke in loud Russian accents and whacked you
on the butt or the tummy if either stuck out. When I
thought of those teachers, my insides froze over. But
you melted the ice with a smile that twisted your nose
to the side—a smile that, thirty years later, is picture-
perfect in my mind.

You patiently helped me move across the floor,
lifting first one knee, then the other, asking me to hop
in between, teaching me to skip. Your compassion

softened a heart already steeled against a dog-eat-dog world filled with public school teachers and coaches who believed that criticism and bullying would frustrate and then compel a student to fight back and work harder.

You exuded compliments and encouragement, positive words said to my mother within earshot of myself: "No one hears the music like she does." My first of several onstage performances was so well rehearsed, that as I stood in the wings, hearing the audience applaud seconds before I was to run onstage, toe to heel, soft arms fluttering behind me, there was no fear of mistakes or failure, only the joy of moving to the music, of bringing the song to life.

You turned an awkward girl into a supple dancer.

Thousands of ballet students passed through your doors over the years. You touched all of their lives, not just mine. We focused and behaved and tried so hard not out of the fear of punishment, but because we loved dance and we loved you.

Years later, when I had my own young children, I read in the paper that you had passed away from cancer. I thought of the physical grace you had bestowed upon me, the trust in other human beings, and my undying love of dance, and I wished I'd written this letter to you years ago.

I may have entered your ballet class with weak feet, but I emerged with my heart strong. And I will strive to emulate your nurturing spirit as I raise my own daughter, who is begging for her first dance lessons this summer.

WITH LOVE AND GRATITUDE,

Indi Zeleny

Monterey Peninsula, California

Indi Zeleny is a Northern California writer/editor. She most recently edited the anthology HerStory, What I Learned in My Bathtub ... and More True Stories on Life, Love, and Other Inconveniences *(Adams Media, 2005).*

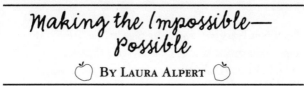

Making the Impossible— Possible

By Laura Alpert

Dear Mrs. Bowen,

The year 1975 was a time before laptop computers and spell-check programs. Through your careful, thoughtful, and patient tutoring, you were able to instill a sense of self-confidence and self-respect that has carried me through my life.

Diagnosed with dyslexia in the sixth grade, I didn't really understand exactly what that meant, but I knew I didn't need a fancy word I could hardly pronounce to tell me that I was a terrible speller.

Every Friday was a nightmare. Every Friday was the spelling test. Every Friday meant tears. Anytime I had a test or a paper returned, slashing red pen marks covered the pages. Each page resembled the remains of a particularly gruesome surgery, in which my blood and guts had been laid out before me. Schoolwork seemed impossible.

The idea of having a language arts class devoted to me and my spelling disability was crushing as well as nauseating. Instead of bounding off to French or Spanish class with the rest of my friends, I came to see you at the Hockaday School in Dallas, Texas, with a chip on my shoulder and butterflies in my stomach.

When I first arrived, you looked up from the worn wooden library table with a smile as warm as the Texas sun. The tiny room was permeated with the fragrance of

Aqua Net hairspray and Rose Garden perfume. I don't remember much of that first day, but I do remember the relief I felt that somehow my frustration with school would subside.

Over time, my spelling improved. You allowed me to do my lessons on a blackboard instead of on paper.

"So I can erase the evidence," I insisted.

No red marks anywhere—on anything I wrote for you. You understood. You patiently coached me on the spelling rules again and again and again.

"*I* before *E* except after *C* unless it sounds like *A,* as in *neighbor* and *weigh.*" Rules I still automatically recite thirty years later.

Fridays became nothing more than the last day of the week. Less and less red ink appeared on my papers. When there was bloodshed, you were always there to bandage the wounds. Because of you, the sight of dreaded red marks no longer excised a pound of flesh. Your gentle graciousness and understanding instilled the belief that I was smart and capable, even with a "learning disability."

"You should never allow anything to stand in your way." These words would be on the blackboard before every class.

At the start of one of our last classes, I casually tossed a rumpled piece of paper I had been clutching for an hour in front of you. "What do you think?" I asked.

You immediately understood the importance of this odd sheet of purple paper. At the top of the page, circled in red, was the magic number—100. I had aced one of the last spelling tests I would ever take. You enveloped me in an enormous rose-scented hug.

"I always knew you could do it" rang in my ears for hours.

With your help the impossible *was* possible.

Armed with a dictionary and the belief that I could excel academically, high school and college awakened a passion for learning. The vocabulary of law school inflicted a few minor cuts and scrapes during exams, but throughout my law practice, I wrote countless pleadings, briefs, and letters, with all the necessary verbiage that encumbers the legal profession.

Now I strive to publish my first novel, a feat never dared dreamed of by this dyslexic student.

I work daily, remembering your words of encouragement and the hours of concentration and preparation. As my spelling improved through practice and diligence, so has my writing. Through it all, your words echo in my thoughts:

"In order to learn from your mistake you must face the mistake, and then address the problem."

I look forward to receiving the 100 percent grade from a publisher someday. I have faith this will happen, because you taught me the impossible is possible.

THANK YOU, MRS. BOWEN, FOR ALL THE POSSIBILITIES IN MY LIFE,

Laura Alpert
Dallas, Texas

Laura Alpert works as a freelance writer, editor, and writing coach. Taking the time to encourage others to achieve their dreams is her passion. A native Dallasite, she is currently tracking down "Big D's" sexiest killer in her latest mystery novel.

Mrs. Heyman's Kindergarten Follies

🍎 By Robin Ehrlichman Woods 🍎

Dear Mrs. Heyman,

I never wanted to go to kindergarten, or leave home at all. I spent my first five years within the loving arms of my family, and when the time came for me to begin school at P.S. 116 in Brooklyn, I was convinced that no one would keep me safe or pamper me ever again. Not only did you make me feel safe, you let me know that I was special. Just how special became evident a few months into the school year.

Kindergarten was a frightening experience for me. I was a shy, apprehensive child who hated being separated from my mommy. You were a kind and patient teacher who tried to get me to stop crying each morning after I begged one last kiss and hug.

You would distract me with barrels full of crayons and colorful paper and by playing beautiful classical music. It seemed the need to be artistic temporarily distracted me from my separation anxiety, enabling nominal participation in class as the tears ran down my chubby cheeks. I also loved to sing and dance, and performed the Virginia Reel when the principal, Mr. Barton, visited our class.

Mr. Barton was an old, stern man who liked to sneak up behind wayward children and shout, "Behave!" I dreaded being the target of his criticism, and practiced the dance with my classmates until you told us we were perfect.

Unfortunately, I was so anxious before Mr. Barton's visit that I wet myself. You calmly took me to the bathroom and gently told me to change into new panties, drying my tears all the while, never showing judgment or sarcasm. My mommy had bought me a gorgeous plaid-and-lace dress for my special performance but had neglected to include an extra set of clothes in case one of my frequent nervous accidents occurred. I blithely removed my wet underpants and put them in a bag inside my cubby. The lack of lingerie did not perturb this five-year-old. My audience awaited, and I had to dance.

My plump body was transformed into a sylphlike prima ballerina's that day as I performed the dance with grace and gusto. Mr. Barton clapped and cheered, bestowing us with one of his rare smiles as he asked us to take a bow. Delighted with his positive response, I bravely stepped up to the front of the classroom and took a deep dramatic bow, throwing wet kisses in your direction.

It was only then that you noticed my naked bottom peeking out for all to see, and tried to persuade me to sit down. Unperturbed and drunk with the power of applause, I turned around and took an unsolicited encore bow. I will never forget Mr. Barton's beet-red face and your paroxysm of laughter. As Mr. Barton made a hasty retreat, eschewing the luscious bakery cookies and cherry Kool-Aid, you bent down and gave me a big hug and kiss, whispering in my ear,

"You've come out of your shell today in more ways than one, my darling."

I was lucky to have you again for the first grade, and learned to love school and the pursuit of learning. You were right about my coming out of my shell and surviving without constant attention from my mommy.

Mrs. Heyman, you were a jewel of a teacher, and I went on to pursue a degree in Early Childhood Education, wanting to be a magical educator just like you. I, too, have seen many tears and bare bottoms over the years, as flashbacks of me emerge in each shy, plump five-year-old who sobs while coloring outside the lines. I also learned to wear slacks each day, as I never know when the urge to dance will come upon me. I will never forget you, my fairy-godmother teacher.

LOVE AND HUGS,

Robin Ehrlichman (Woods)
Montclair, New Jersey

After briefly considering a career in dance, Robin Ehrlichman Woods realized that her true calling was teaching. She writes for women's, parenting, and humor publications, and enjoys pirouetting barefoot through the rain.

Ready, Set, Go!

🍎 BY CASEY MEEHAN 🍎

Dear Mrs. Valentine,

Thank you for being one of the most understanding teachers ever. In third grade you taught not only me, but the whole class to be sincere, well tempered, intelligent, good children. In your class, I learned ethics—not just intelligence. You had the ability to teach in a fun, specific style that kept the whole class interested and organized. You also helped with my stress habits, keeping my nervous self from harming me. You could also keep all of the kids happy and from fighting because of your skill to break up conflict.

Throughout the whole year, you taught the class several things. When we worked with plants, your great knowledge of them taught the class details that we will always remember. I still remember my obsession with cows, which I still question myself about today. You taught the class non-third grade material too, such as spiritual ways, and ways with our own emotions. One thing that I enjoyed learning especially in your class was about spiders, which turned out to be fascinating.

Thanks Mrs. Valentine, for when I left your class I was a better person.

SINCERELY,

Casey Meehan

Los Angeles, California

Casey Meehan is a twelve-year-old growing up in Los Angeles, California. He used to want to be a chemist, then a rocket scientist, and is now thinking about becoming a medical researcher.

Stepping into the Light

By Adrienne Small

Dear Mrs. Weinstein,

I'm so glad I don't have to see my dad anymore. If it weren't for you, I would still be seeing him, despite all the things he has done to me in the past. I've had such a hard time this school year, and just wanted to thank you whole-heartedly for everything you have done.

I know I haven't been the simplest person to contend with, but you went through with it even though there were so many others who said I was doomed to failure. There is no way I could ever pay you back for all you've done for me.

Despite my dreadful attendance and endless emotional predicaments, you always had hope for me—and I'm still not sure why. You've taught me that no matter what you have done in your life, you always have a chance. No textbook could have ever taught me that!

I realize that you think you've done little, but you've actually changed my entire life just by being there for me. After the past abuse from my father, I thought that my life was bleak, but you made me stop and appreciate what I have and all that I had previously taken for granted.

I always thought that teachers were flawless; that they were picture perfect and merciless. After meeting you, I learned that teachers are just the same as anyone else. In fact, some of them have more in common with me than I would have ever believed.

It was because of you that I faced my fears and finally got off my medication. In truth, if it wasn't for you, I might not even still be alive today. I would have probably given up without you always being there to encourage me and keep me going. I would say that the greatest lesson you taught me was that I am worth love and respect.

Thank you, sincerely, for everything you've done. I will never forget you or your compassion, and neither will my family. What you have done for me and countless other students is astonishing. Next year, I will miss you and remember everything you have taught me this past year. Unfortunately, since I will not be going to Berks Career and Technology Center next year, I will probably never see you again. But I wish you the best of luck and offer my infinite gratitude for everything.

And Mrs. Weinstein, you should know that I am not the only student who is so very grateful for what you have done for them. I know several students, like me, who also consider you their hero. Do not think of this letter as being only from me, but as a letter from every student you've ever aided.

I know most students don't say anything to you personally, but they certainly do mention you when they are with their friends. It's so strange how you can meet someone who changes your life forever and you don't even realize it. In my life, Mrs. Weinstein, you are that person.

Thank you!

YOUR STUDENT,

Adrienne Small

Wernersville, Pennsylvania

Adrienne Small is a sixteen-year-old high school junior from Wernersville, Pennsylvania. Her life's ambition is to become a writer/journalist.

The Silk Wedding Gown

🍎 BY VICKI H. NELSON 🍎

Dear Mrs. Easley,

It's been over thirty years since I was in the seventh grade, but the memories of junior high will be with me forever. Most kids enter junior high with a certain amount of anxiety—but I was terrified. In my uneducated family, I was led to believe that school was insignificant, and when I heard how hard those years would be, I felt I would never make it. But you saw through my insecurities. You recognized that I lacked confidence and self-esteem and you did something about it.

We had to write many papers in your English class at South Junior High in Hopkins, Minnesota, and the projects you gave us required brainstorming. During one project, you put me in charge of my group, and I really wondered about you at that point. What were you thinking? I didn't know how to give orders!

Our class was to put on a production of *The Wizard of Oz* for a neighborhood elementary school. When you assigned me the role of Glinda the Good Witch of the North, I remember thinking you were nuts. I knew I could *never* stand in front of a group of kids—no matter if they were younger than I—and utter even two words.

I was scared out of my mind.

But then you brought a dress for me to wear in the play, and it wasn't just any old dress. It had been your wedding dress. I couldn't believe you trusted me to wear your silk gown! It was exactly the boost I needed. My voice may not have been booming during the play, but my heart was soaring. I flew in the clouds till the end of the year. Not only had you given me a sense of confidence I had never felt, you gave me a sense of worth I had never had.

The next fall I would be in the eighth grade. After you announced that you would be teaching eighth grade the next year, you took me aside and told me you had requested that I be in your class. I had no words for you. Other than my grandmother, I didn't have anyone in my life who made me feel wanted.

I entered eighth grade a little more excited. We learned to write poems that year. You read one of my poems to the class, and later, you asked me if you could keep that poem as an example to read to future classes. Of course, I said yes. Do you know I can still recite a portion of that poem?

That same year, the theater group you were in put on the play *Fiddler on the Roof,* and you invited my family to watch the performance. Until then, I'd never experienced the theater, but to this day, I love to attend plays and have passed that love on to my own family.

In your classroom, I acquired knowledge of the English language, but more importantly, I acquired a love of learning. I entered ninth grade with courage and excitement, and when it came time for senior high, I was ready. I was confident and self-assured. I made many friends, and thoroughly enjoyed my senior high years.

Mrs. Easley, because you believed in me, I have experienced many accomplishments. I worked my way up to a leadership position in an insurance company, I homeschooled my son through his senior year, and two years ago, I published my first short story.

A frightened little girl first put on that silk wedding gown, but a confident little girl emerged from it.

THANK YOU FOR TAKING THE TIME TO CARE.
SINCERELY,

Vicki Nelson
Beaverton, Oregon

Vicki H. Nelson grew up in Minnesota. A writer and avid reader, she now resides in Oregon with her husband and two sons.

Learning to Walk

☙ By Everett Gavel ☙

Hello Rosey,

I was twenty-three years old, living in Tampa Bay, Florida, when I lost my sight. I'm finally writing to you to express my feelings of love and gratitude for all you did for me those many years ago. Thankfully, I found you at the Pinellas Center for the Visually Impaired, in the nearby city of Largo. You helped me gain back my independence—and my life.

Although more than a decade has passed since I was under your tutelage, I think of you and your Orientation and Mobility lessons every time I walk past a tree or pole that's in the section of sidewalk between the street and me. You taught me to simply pay attention to what's going on around me, like noticing the split second where those thin barriers block the sound coming from the street.

I can no longer see the obstacles or scenery, but thanks to all you taught me in that short time, I now usually "sense" the item's being there as I pass by. I remember when I was under your training and you were trying to explain that point—I thought you were nuts. Now it all seems so natural.

The ability to push past my fear was gained due to my knowing you were not far off if I needed you. My ability to get past my pride and ask for help if I needed it was gained while learning from you, listening to you, and growing under your guidance.

I remember many things you told me that I didn't realize I'd retained until years later. Things like walking past telephone poles, or lightly tapping my cane at about shoulder's width, rather than swinging it like a scythe, as I did in the very beginning. Thanks to you I learned to recover quickly (most times) and stop abruptly if my cane suddenly fell off into oblivion, losing touch with the sidewalk. The loss of contact may well indicate an open sewer, manhole cover, or construction site, but is, of course, most often merely the curb dropping down to a side or cross street. I've learned to watch that first step. As they say, it can be a doozy. However, you trained me properly and competently, so I no longer let those things hold me back.

I clearly remember my final Orientation and Mobility test, traversing the cityscape of Largo entirely on my own to meet you for lunch at Chi-Chi's restaurant. I recall walking through the door, smelling the aroma of fajitas, and hearing the sizzling meat in those cast-iron serving pans as waiters brought meals to tables. The fried ice cream was never better than during our meal that afternoon. I felt so competent and capable as I walked through the front door that day, knowing you had helped me learn to get there on my own.

Thanks to your efforts, I'm unafraid to venture out on my own now, even when traveling in a new city. You gave me the understanding and courage to simply "get the job done," no matter the supposed obstacles. You taught me—undeniably—that I can be dropped off anywhere, not even knowing exactly where, and still find the location where I need to go.

Thanks to you, dear Rosey, I enjoy life. I once again regularly enjoy things I long ago took for granted, such as going out to eat, or shopping. I'm participating again in sports and outdoor activities that I avoided for a while. I enjoy volunteering, helping others, going to church, going to my kids' school events, and numerous other things. All thanks to you, and to the cane-travel skills you taught me.

Over the last decade, working as an advocate for those dealing with vision loss, I've met too many people living sad, lonely lives because they've succumbed to their disability. I'm thankful you helped me avoid that trap. By doing so, you've allowed me to truly live, rather than be hindered by fear.

Thank you, Rosey, for giving me the chance and the ability to thrive, rather than merely survive.

SINCERELY, AND WITH LOVE,
ALWAYS YOUR STUDENT AND
ALWAYS YOUR FRIEND,

Everett Gavel
Barberton, Ohio

Everett Gavel is a freelance nonfiction writer who can be reached at www.everettgavel.com. *His favorite thing in life is being daddy to his two daughters, and he works in the assistive technology field, helping blind and low-vision computer users achieve success.*

Red Ink in a Journal

🍎 By Melanie Stiles 🍎

Dear Mrs. Bentley,

I've often wondered if the requirement for all students in Senior English to keep a daily journal originally came from you. My classmates and I wrote on the most insignificant subjects we could dream up. This, of course, was a mass decision based on the pecking order as we understood it. We determined never to let you in on even the miniscule aspects of our lives. No, not a teacher . . . that would be unforgivable.

As such, I stayed true to my peers, struggling far too long to stretch the boring and mundane into a minimum one-page entry. That is, until she died.

Quite unexpectedly (at least to me), I lost my mother. The diagnosis of multiple sclerosis was handed down eight years before, along with a life expectancy of a mere four years. Somehow, I'd convinced myself back in year five or six that she was here to stay. The shock of her passing was almost unbearable.

Your mandated journal became a place to put my pain, my anger, my unappeased grief. I wrote to you about the upturned casket handle. I forced my best friend to go up and fix it before the service started. I admitted to you, and only you, that I was alone with my mother in the hospital room when she stopped breathing, and how I ran into the corridor, screaming for help. I even included the worst of it all—watching her eyes fade to blankness while my empty outstretched arms yearned to bring her back. All my tear-stained admissions poured out on those pages—the same pages I turned in once a week for grading.

My secret desire? That you would challenge my newly skewed viewpoints on life, love, and God. I desperately needed somewhere to channel my emotions. You stepped up to the task, but in an unforeseeable way—you had also lost your own mother too soon.

You bled your comfort and wisdom onto my pages. Your pen, a beacon, walked me through the murky corridors of my misery. I now realize you had to revisit that little girl's pain inside you to respond in such a manner. For that, I thank you profusely.

The class of 1975 at Ebert L. Furr High School in Houston, Texas, considered you the strictest teacher on the faculty. Upon returning from Christmas break, you gave every student three raps on the palm of the hand because none of us did our homework over the holidays. Thirty years later, the sting of that ruler seems unremarkable. But red ink in the margin of a journal is still crystal clear in my mind.

GOD BLESS YOU.

Melanie
Cypress, Texas

Melanie Stiles uses her background to share joys, hardships, and other life journeys with her fellow man. She has accumulated more than 130 bylines in various publications.

Summertime

🍎 BY KAYLA HOLCOMB 🍎

Dear Mrs. Watts,

You are my favorite teacher in the whole wide world. I will miss you over summer vacation. I had a whole lot of fun with you in second grade. You are very special to me because you are very nice, kind, sweet and very loveaBle. I had a lot of fun with you and Mr. Stiner. I hope you have a wonderful summer vacatio and I will see you in The fall.

love,
Kayla Holcom

Poland, Ohio

Kayla Holcomb is a nine-year-old from Poland, Ohio. She loves playing soccer, swimming, and horseback riding.

Destination Unknown

🍎 By Suzan L. Wiener 🍎

Dear Ms. St. John,

I always looked up to you because not only were you beautiful on the outside, you were beautiful on the inside. I was the nerdy fifth grader who was overweight and wore glasses, and I wasn't part of the popular crowd at Public School 13 in the Bronx.

You saw how other students treated me—teasing and bumping into me on purpose. Whenever you were aware of what was going on, you stopped it cold. You'd take my hand and say, "Susie, I need you to help me grade their papers."

That made them take notice and realize I mattered!

I don't think you were aware of just how special I thought you were for doing that, and all the other kind deeds you bestowed upon me. You never asked for anything in return. You were doing it to help a child in need and I am forever grateful.

On several Saturdays you even came to my house and took me for a delicious ice-cream sundae—my favorite—because you knew my mother was busy with my sister and cleaning the house. I loved being with you. We joked and laughed, and you seemed to enjoy it as much as I did. I don't think you were pretending either. It made me so happy knowing you were my special friend.

I remember when the music teacher announced we would have a piano recital. I knew immediately I wanted to play *Destination Unknown,* the original song that you wrote the lyrics to. What a wonderful song! I know it by heart to this day.

"I go for a stroll, there's nothing to do, my mind's in a whirl, just thinking of you. . . ."

When the day of the recital arrived, I was quite nervous, but you tried to calm me, telling me not to worry. You said everybody was rooting for me, but I knew that wasn't true. Some of the other students wanted me to fail. I almost didn't succeed, but you helped me be a winner.

When I sat down to play—I froze. My fingers didn't want to touch the keys, as if they had a mind of their own. Staring out at the audience made me so nervous, and the butterflies in my stomach started fluttering to the point I could hear them flapping.

Of course you noticed right away what was happening, and you didn't let me down. You came to my rescue, sat down, patted my hand, and whispered, "Susie, you play the right hand and I'll play the left."

We finished to a standing ovation, and I felt so proud that you were in my corner. I will never forget how much that meant to me, Ms. St. John.

Over the years, you had given me so much, and in doing so, you taught me that giving of yourself is the most important lesson of all.

Today, when you are looking down at me from heaven, and I'm playing *Destination Unknown* as an adult who's so grateful to you for helping to make me who I am, I know you are smiling at me. I think of that little child whom you aided in her time of need, and I smile too, because you have touched my heart in more ways than one.

THANK YOU, MS. ST. JOHN, FOR BEING YOU. WITH LOVE,

Suzan
Spring Hill, Florida

Suzan L. Wiener has published numerous poems, stories, articles, and shorter pieces in Mature Living, Saturday Evening Post, Verses, Poetry Press *(first prize),* NEB Publishing *(first prize). Her love poetry e-book is at Lionsong Publications,* http://lspbookstore.netfirms.com/fiction/poetry.htm

Bluebells and the Blessed Virgin

By Phil Young

Dear Sister Agatha,

You won't remember me, as it's been a long, long time since our paths crossed at the convent school in West Cork, Ireland. However, my thoughts frequently slip back to the time when I was ten years old, and you were the much feared head teacher of our primary school.

I was a shy youngster who, for some reason, always felt at a disadvantage amongst my fellow students. You were a bit of a fearsome presence—a nun whose knowledge was awesome, whose teaching methods were unorthodox, and whose outlook was broad during an era that was oppressive. In the late '40s, literature was censored, cinema cut, and foreign ideas frowned upon.

You, however, encouraged your young students to read newspapers, listen to radio, and appreciate good writing. You also encouraged us to look at the world around us, and to rejoice in the beauty of everyday things—birdsong, clouds racing across a winter sky, the light and shadow on a cornfield.

One event in particular stands clear in my memory. It was May, the month of Mary, mother of God, and each classroom had an altar in her honor. We were encouraged to adorn the altar with flowers and plants, so on the following morning, I arose with the dawn and rushed to the woods behind our house. There I picked an armful of wild bluebells. Wrapping my offering in newspaper, I made my way to school.

When I arrived, I was met with hoots of laughter. "Wildflowers! Weeds! You don't think Sister will let you put those on the altar, do you?" My classmates had come to school bearing potted geraniums and shop-bought carnations.

Burning with shame, I was about to slink out to deposit my treasure in the bin, when you, Sister, entered. You immediately sensed the situation. Taking my bundle from me, you chose the nicest vase and arranged my contribution before the statue of the Blessed Virgin.

"So perfect!" you exclaimed, burying your face in the scented freshness of the bluebells. "Our Lady will be especially pleased that you picked these for her."

Thanks to you, my flowers held a place of pride on that altar. I learned an important lesson from your handling of that situation. I learned to have confidence in my own judgment, my own way of doing things. Some years after I had moved on from your class, I heard that you had left the convent—a courageous choice in those days. I hope that for you it was a decision that brought you contentment and happiness.

YOUR PAST PUPIL,

Philomena Young
Dublin, Ireland

Phil Young is a native of Cork in Ireland. She is married to Keith, a Welshman; is a mother of four, grandmother of five; and loves reading, gardening, walking, and traveling.

2. You Made Me a Better Person

Human beings, by their very nature, are in a constant search for ways to better themselves. Sometimes, the road to personal enlightenment is a smooth ride through enchanted scenery filled with whimsy and wonder. Other times, the road winds dangerously through treacherous terrain.

No matter which road you traverse, it's certain that along the way, you learn something that will ultimately make you better prepared for future journeys. Teachers are the milestones that mark our roads. They provide respite and give us pause to reflect on our betterment, the individuals we are, and the individuals we hope to become. They nurture our souls, rekindle our flames, encourage our creativity and actions, and draw from us our hidden potential.

Teachers make us better individuals, and in doing so, pave the way for a world filled with thoughtful, caring, intelligent inhabitants who make us proud to be alive.

A Beautiful Drowned Rat

🍎 By Karen Noblitt 🍎

Dear Sister Kathy,

Of all my years in school, the six that I spent in Catholic school stand out the most in my memory. I can still remember that summer day in 1985 in Old Bridge, New Jersey. It was the first day of school, and as I rode the bus that warm morning, I was nervous. Tightly clutching my book bag, I bent my head and prayed that this year would be different. Maybe—just maybe—I could be accepted instead of picked on. Maybe some of my classmates had grown over summer vacation and I wouldn't be the tallest one in class anymore.

The bus pulled up to the school and we all jumped out, excited to see friends we'd missed during the past three months. As I made my way to the cluster of kids playing together under the big white handwritten sign that read *Fifth Grade,* I saw that my prayers would not be answered. I was still the tallest, looming over everyone like a giant. Feeling sudden dread for the upcoming year, I sat Indian-style on the hot concrete, elbows on my knees, head in my hands.

"Hey, Karen, come see the lake behind the school—it's full of frogs!" called a familiar voice from behind me. Anxious about what might be in store for me, but desperate to fit in, I jumped to my feet and followed the crowd to the lake. Once there, I noticed students throwing pebbles into the lake, some standing on rocks close to the water.

"You can't see from all the way back here, follow me!" instructed a girl who was in my class last year—a girl who pushed me into the boy's restroom on the last day of school. She grabbed my hand and brought me to the water's edge. Trying hard to keep my balance, I suddenly felt a hard shove from behind!

Before I knew what had happened, I was sitting in the lake, my uniform skirt a big bubble around my thighs. Laughter surrounded me as hot tears flowed from my eyes. *"Look at the jolly green giant! Look at the jolly green giant!"* Over and over again they hurled insults, until, mercifully, the bell rang.

Walking slowly and dripping wet, I made my way toward the school. Once inside, I went to the fifth-grade classrooms and found the list of who was in which teacher's class. My heart sank! There was my name listed under your classroom—the strictest teacher in the entire school. What would you say when I entered your classroom looking like a drowned rat?

Before I had a chance to find out, the door opened and there you stood, ready to take the class to morning bathroom break. Before I could explain why I was late, you instructed the class to return to their seats and came out into the hall with me, closing the door behind you. You knelt down, gathered me into your arms and wiped my wet hair from my eyes. Sobs racked my body as you held me close.

"They pushed me into the lake," I sputtered between labored breaths. Pulling me back so that I was standing before you, you held both my hands in yours. "Do you know what I would change about you?" you asked me softly. I shook my head. "Nothing," you replied. "God made you beautiful, and if I was a little girl, I would want to look just like you."

Stunned, my mouth hung open and my eyes grew big.

"The other kids want to look just like you too. They make fun of you because they envy how tall you are, your pretty hair, and the way your eyes light up when you smile. They figure that if they make fun of you, others won't notice that they don't fit in as well as they would like."

Sister Kathy, I never did tell you this on the first day of school, but thank you! You reached out and encouraged a girl who desperately needed someone to notice how beautiful she really was. Sometimes I still struggle with my differences, but I remember our little talk and silently know that others in the world don't fit in as well as they would like to either. I want you to know that all these years later, you still make a difference.

FOREVER GRATEFUL,

Karen Noblitt
Wallis, Texas

Karen Noblitt is married and is a stay-at-home mom to three children.

Eyes Wide Open

BY CHERISE WYNEKEN

Dear Miss H.,

I still can't call you Millicent, like some of the gals do now. Especially not, Miss Hamburger. To me, you'll always be "Miss H.," as we affectionately called you at Acalanes High in Lafayette, California, during the early 1940s. Most of the students knew you through your English classes, but we girls loved you most for your role as leader of the extracurricular activity—modern dance à la Elizabeth Duncan, as you always pointed out.

A lovely woman with striking black hair and a lithe, slender body, you taught us how to move our bodies gracefully, to hear stories and see movements in music, and to create and choreograph. We gained self-confidence through your acceptance and encouragement as we performed before an audience at spring and fall concerts, and our appreciation of music grew as we danced to Hungarian Rhapsody no. 2, "Go Down Moses," or Tchaikovsky's "Sleeping Beauty Waltz." Dance brought aspects of our subconscious out from behind our ego masks and let them move and be exposed.

But it was in your English class that I learned the most valuable lesson you offered. "I'm going to read you an article on anti-Semitism," you said to our class one day. "Then I want you to write a paper discussing it." I had never heard that term before, and didn't have a clue what it meant. The article spoke of Hitler's aggrandizement of blond, blue-eyed Aryans above other races; of pogroms, ghettos, and discrimination involving Jews. I had been brought up in a Christian setting, sent to Sunday school, and studied Bible stories. To me the word *Jew* simply meant God's people in Old Testament times. Why should they be treated badly?

That day, seated at a wooden desk in a small classroom, my eyes were opened to the horror of racism. My innocent world of family, friends, music, and dance was suddenly expanded to include sounds of suffering from people outside my little circle. I strongly defended the Jews in my essay.

Just as dance brought out my feelings, your introduction to prejudice was a stepping-stone to inclusiveness. Your lesson, assimilated at a formative age, helped me deal with relationships and ethnic differences in creative ways. Ultimately, I gained an international family: an African American son-in-law, a Mexican American son-in-law, a Jewish daughter-in-law, and even an Episcopalian (I was brought up Lutheran). You wove patterns of tolerance into my life, allowing me to celebrate and appreciate the variety in my expanding family.

Even on into your nineties, you challenged and inspired us by your continued attendance and participation at our annual dance reunions, letting us know that age should never deter us from following our dreams. The picture taken on your 100th birthday, with you seated on an exercise bicycle, arms splayed high in a vee, was your farewell gift to us. Thank you, Miss H.; thank you for everything.

YOUR STUDENT AND FRIEND,

Cherise
Albany, California

Cherise Wyneken is a freelance writer whose prose and poetry have appeared in a variety of journals, periodicals, anthologies, two books of poetry, and her memoir, Round Trip.

Quarky and Quirky in the Cosmos

 By ALEXANDRA PAJAK

Dear Mr. Grimes,

The morning you threw yourself on the ground in playful convulsions to demonstrate hyperactivity in atoms, I knew you weren't the usual high school science teacher. I admit I didn't know what to think at the time, but I do know this—I still remember that life is full of things to learn about, and that electrons can become excited, combine with other substances, and are full of energy. The very things that life is made of move constantly, never stop, and constantly change.

Your unique insight taught us to live as keen observers of both science and life. The second day of class you asked us to list, on a sheet of scrap paper, seven things you wore the first day of class. Among them: a Band-Aid on your right ring finger, a wedding ring on your left ring finger, a colorful tie, and sneakers instead of loafers. "Observation is the key to being a scientist," you said. "Whether we want to enter science, the FBI, or teaching, we must learn to watch and learn from our environment and from those around us."

You also ensured that each of us understood chemical and physical properties of life through your grueling weekly quizzes. Always printed on a single page, the quizzes challenged me greatly, and I never fully appreciated the work that went into writing and taking the quizzes until my first chemistry course in college. I aced the first exam, which contained much of the information you taught us in general chemistry in eleventh grade.

You inspired me to change, Mr. Grimes. I wasn't very popular in school, and I used to work extra hard on homework, aiming for a scholarship to go to a good college where I'd be happy. I sometimes stayed up until three or four o'clock in the morning, which I now recognize as unhealthy. In your class after one of those nights, I accidentally spilled a bottle of sulfuric acid on myself in your chemistry lab. The acid splattered on my pants, tore the cloth, and reached my skin. You calmly instructed me to go to the restroom immediately and rinse myself of the chemical.

Later that week, I told you after class that my tiredness most likely contributed to that day's mishap. Your voice was soft and fatherly as you told me, "You don't need to do that. No one needs to stay up that late studying." I never have since, and I thank you for helping me to take better care of myself and to reassess my priorities.

You also encouraged me to hold on to my religious faith in God, despite advances in science that resulted in cynicism toward religion. You described in class how electrons jump from energy level to energy level, disappearing for an instant only to appear in another level the next. On the subject of physical reality, you said, "I believe in God. I believe God made rules in the universe, but that God sometimes breaks them."

You also challenged me to break the rules. You encouraged each of the five female students in your senior physics class to excel just as much as you encouraged the twenty-five male students also in the course. Immediately after college, I entered a Ph.D. program at Georgia Tech. I have teachers like you to thank for the inspiration and self-assurance that brought me where I am today; not only as a student, but as a confident human being.

Let this letter be my fit of energy, my excitement for life, and my thanks for your wisdom. You taught us well, Mr. Grimes. Thank you.

SINCERELY,

Alexandra Pajak
Atlanta, Georgia

Alexandra Pajak is currently pursuing a Ph.D. in the History of Technology and Society at Georgia Tech. Her essays, poems, and plays appear in What We Think: Young Voters Speak Out, Our Time Is Now, Agnes Scott Writers Festival *magazine, and* Contemporary Topics in Laboratory Animal Medicine.

The Teacher's Chair

🍎 By Joshua Vogt 🍎

Dear Mrs. Welton,

I remember you perched on a director's chair at the front of our fourth-grade class. It was 1991 at Rocky Bayou Christian School in Niceville, Florida, and no one *ever* sat in that chair but you.

You peered at me with disapproval, as I had already disrupted the class twice with what you called "smart-alecky" comments.

"This is boring," I complained, sliding my arms along the desk and leaning my head to the side to emphasize my weariness.

You raised a thin eyebrow. "Perhaps you would rather come up and teach the class yourself?"

The offer struck me with motivation and wonder. Eight years old and not understanding the concept of sarcasm, I jumped out of my seat and ran up to where you sat in front of the green chalkboard. I turned and faced the class as they watched with wide eyes and wider grins as I took up the challenge.

You cocked your head in consideration, not expecting me to respond as I did. I paused, fearing you didn't mean the invitation and would send me trudging in shame back down the rows between my sniggering classmates.

In the silence, someone dropped a pencil. It clattered and rolled, but no one picked it up. Then you stood and walked over to your desk in the corner of the room. You left your teaching manual open to pages that explained the cotton gin and the Industrial Revolution.

I shuffled over to the chair and pulled myself up onto it. Dragging the heavy book into my lap to hide my trembling hands, I began to teach.

To this day, I can't recall what I said. It came out a mix of what I caught in covert peeks at the manual and my own imaginings of history. I always thought my versions were more interesting anyway. The class listened in rare silence. Several times I stumbled over awkward names and large words, and you prompted me from the sidelines until I pronounced them correctly.

When the class bell rang, I clambered down from the chair and returned to my seat amid giggles and congratulatory pokes from my friends. You watched me as I went, and nodded your head in solemn thanks.

"Class dismissed," you said. "No homework for tomorrow since the teacher forgot to assign any."

It was years later when I heard your opinion of my efforts. Apparently you'd spoken to my mother later that day when she picked me up from school.

"He did pretty well," you told her.

During that class period, you gave me the lifelong ability to stand in front of others without fear of who I am. You helped me realize what it felt like to instill knowledge into the minds of others using words and imagination.

Mrs. Welton, you taught out of true concern for our education, but even more, you nurtured the dreams of a room full of rowdy fourth graders—even those who went out of their way to disrupt the lessons with spit wads and note passing.

You taught best by letting me teach.

ALWAYS WITH THANKS,

Joshua Vogt
Denver, Colorado

Joshua Vogt lives in Colorado and recently graduated with a bachelor of arts from Colorado Christian University.

Stand Tall

By Jewell Johnson

Dear Mrs. Roberts,

I don't remember much about eighth grade or the physical education class you taught at Kennedy Community School in Minnesota in 1947. I can't tell you what color gym shorts and T-shirts we wore or the games we played or if we did jumping jacks or stretching exercises. And the rules for volleyball and softball still escape me. But I often recall what you said to me one day during one of those classes, because your words so changed my attitude that I have never forgotten them. Now, as a grandmother, I realize what you said forever affected me emotionally, spiritually, and physically.

You may not have known that at age thirteen I was painfully aware of my height. I was at least five inches taller than all the boys in eighth grade, and I was also very thin. Not knowing how sensitive I was about my tall, skinny frame, people often called me "Beanpole." They were joking, but the name hurt. How I longed to be short like my friends Marilyn and Joanne!

"I may be tall," I reasoned to myself, "but I won't be *that* tall."

In an effort to appear shorter, I began to walk with slouched shoulders and buckled knees. Whenever there was a wall nearby, I'd lean on it. I would often sit hunched over at my desk or slide down on my spine. Anything not to be tall.

Then came that day in P.E. class when the students were weighed and measured. In turn, each girl would stand on the scale. You'd weigh us and place the rod on our heads to measure our height. In a loud voice, you'd then announce the information for the secretary to record.

How I dreaded that day! *When Mrs. Roberts announces my height,* I thought, *everyone will know exactly how tall I am.* How horrible! I imagined the short girls twittering, "Did you hear how tall she is? Wow! That's tall!"

When the dreaded time came for me to be measured, I cleverly buckled my knees, hunched my shoulders, and waited for the bad news. But instead of lining me up to the measuring stick, you paused.

"Dear," you whispered so the others wouldn't hear, "you're beginning to slouch. Put your shoulders back. Stand tall. Be proud of yourself." Then you gave me a reassuring smile.

No, Mrs. Roberts, I don't remember much about that class, but all my life I've been thankful for the teacher who took time to see into an awkward teenager's heart and say words that changed her life. I'm a better person today because of what you said, and I pray I will be as sensitive and discerning of the needs of others as you were to me that day. Thank you.

SINCERELY,

Jewell Johnson
Fountain Hills, Arizona

Jewell Johnson lives in Arizona with her husband, LeRoy. They are parents to six children and grandparents to eight. Besides writing, Jewell spends her time reading, walking, and quilting.

Wrapped in Flannel PJ's

🍎 BY ANITA HIGMAN 🍎

Dear Mrs. Brymore,

As you probably remember, the hallways in our rural western Oklahoma high school in the '70s were highly charged with teenage angst. My own anxiety at being alive at sixteen was compounded with a slight weight problem, heavy eyeglasses, acne, and poor self-esteem. Those years represented a coming-of-age scene that didn't delight all those in attendance.

Then you entered my school life. Being around you was like being wrapped in flannel pj's—warm and comforting. I could feel your smile coming before you entered a classroom. Your laughter was free flowing, like a kite released in a breeze. I can't remember how you looked with a frown, though surely you had one at some point! With your caring attitude and camaraderie, I knew we were more than students. We were precious folk you genuinely liked to be around.

I recall how trustworthy you were and how you fostered that quality in others. One summer, you rescued me from some miserable waitressing work by offering me a job as your helper at the school's library as it was being revamped. You gave me my instructions, made sure I was comfortable with them, and then never once glared over my shoulder as if waiting for me to fail. Your eyes always said, "I know you can do this, Anita." You placed more confidence in me than I did in myself. What a boost that summer was to the faltering ego of a lip-chewing teenager.

I also remember your compassionate truths. Your advice ranged from the profound to the practical. Once, when I was trying to impress a young man, you mentioned how wise it would be to remove the gum from my mouth. Apparently, in my fervor to claim his affection, I'd created an open-mouthed smacking commotion that could be experienced from quite a distance. I thanked you for your keen observations and quickly removed my gum.

As I reflect on your life as an educator, I'd like to think I figured out your most basic secret—you always went that extra mile. You didn't just instruct, you nurtured. You never punished, but instead guided with caring discipline. You didn't just watch over students, you loved them. The gathering of knowledge was important, and the classroom time necessary, but your willingness to go beyond books with a sincere, serving attitude was even more vital.

Without you in my formative years, I may have drifted, grown weary, or simply given up my goals. Your influence in my life is not a onetime story or the telling of a crossroads moment, but one of molding the angst of a teenager into good and lovely qualities, which you helped to arrange each day into the mosaic of what I dreamed to become.

With this letter, I thank you for your patience, your truthfulness, your laughter, your guidance, and your love. They will never be forgotten.

MOST SINCERELY,

Anita Higman
Tomball, Texas

Award-winning author Anita Higman has published seventeen books for children and adults and is a contributor to seven nonfiction compilations. Her Web site is www.anitahigman.com.

Life Lessons in the Classroom

🍎 By Veronica H. Free 🍎

Dear Mrs. Payne,

What did you ever do with that large papier-mâché dinosaur you let us create in the basement of your home the year I was in your fourth-grade classroom? That was certainly a memorable experience, one of many wonderful memories I have of being one of your students. Not only did you teach me the necessary academics that year, you also taught me many valuable life lessons.

Although it has been more than thirty years since I sat in your classroom in Park Street Elementary School in Asheboro, North Carolina, the life lessons you taught me still apply today. I was too young at the time to realize how valuable these lessons were, but as I continued through school and progressed to adulthood, I became more aware of what a wise teacher you were.

Whether by fate, divine intervention, or due process of class assignment, being placed under your tutelage was the best thing that could have happened to a quiet, shy, insecure fourth grader. You accepted me as I was without trying to reshape me. You made me feel special and never made me uncomfortable in any situation. Acceptance is a quality I learned from you, and it's an important part of my life as an adult. I have no right to judge others or attempt to change them. It is best to accept them as they are.

Each day, you entered the classroom with a smile. You proved the theory to be true that a calm, soft voice gains more respect than a loud, angry voice. Having the patience to allow us to come into your basement and create that awesome dinosaur demonstrated your willingness to go beyond the perimeter and encourage our creativity. You wanted learning to be fun for us, and it was.

I have always loved animals and found solace in their companionship, and this love of animals seemed to strengthen the bond between us. You allowed your students to experience the wonders of nature firsthand. One day, you brought a box that held several furry bundles of joy just waiting to be loved into the classroom. I was one of the children fortunate enough to be able to take home a tiny black-and-white kitten.

Looking back, I believe you knew how much I needed that kitten to love, and you must have done some behind-the-scenes persuading in order for my parents to allow me to take it home. That kitten brought a tremendous amount of joy into my life.

Your approach to teaching involved getting to know each of your students, their families, and their individual situations. After moving on from your class, I returned to visit you often, as did many of your students. Each time I visited, you welcomed me with a smile and a hug. If I saw you outside of school, you were always friendly and concerned about how things were going for me.

As an adult I realize what a good role model you were for me, and I'm thankful for the life lessons I learned from you. There are many good educators who provide academic training, but you were an excellent teacher. Along with what I learned from books, I learned by example the qualities I needed to develop in order to have a positive impact on others throughout my life. Each day you demonstrated acceptance, patience, kindness, and understanding. You taught me to value others and accept their differences. I learned from you the importance of protecting and respecting nature.

Years after leaving your classroom, my memories remain vivid. I think of you more often than I think of any other teacher I've had. I sincerely appreciate all that you taught me, and I wish all children could have at least one teacher like you in their lives.

SINCERELY,

Veronica
Asheboro, North Carolina

Veronica H. Free is a published poet and writer with a desire to inspire and comfort others with her writing. She enjoys the stillness of rural living. Her passion is caring for her retired greyhounds.

The Crying Towel

🍎 By Dana Smith-Mansell 🍎

Dear Dr. Maxis,

It's been a few years since we locked horns, but I have never forgotten you. Your class and instructional methods left an indelible impression. In a tribute that only you can appreciate—I don't know whether to thank you or flatten your tires.

It was a summer in the late 1980s, and I was taking my final class with you to complete my master's degree in education. I was anxious about graduation and the successful completion of your class.

As luck would have it, we were like kindred spirits when class started. You enjoyed bouncing questions and posing hypotheses to me, and seemed to welcome my responses. I was settling in and feeling comfortable until I did the unthinkable . . .

I disagreed with a statement you made.

From that point on, my quizzes and assignments seemed substandard in your eyes. You took every opportunity to let me and the entire class know that I should know the correct answer—*your* answer—to every question you posed.

Our interactions became a game, and as the class continued, I often flashed back to an undergrad professor I'd had years earlier, who had similar combative teaching methods. Like you, she would ask an open-ended question that required a personal response, and then proceed to nail me to the wall.

I recalled what I'd learned from that previous professor, and formulated a plan of attack. Ego has its merit, but nobody's *that* good. Being that I was too much of a lady to flatten anyone's tires, much less a professor's, I decided on a revenge more cerebral. As such, I ignored you, and set my mind on the ultimate prize—your final exam.

Because you continually told the class how brutal it would be, and how rarely ("never") anyone received an A, I thought it would be my crowning moment. So, I sat through your criticisms, read your bold red marks written with disdain on my papers, and waited.

Did I mention you taught me patience?

When the day of your final arrived, I was ready. As you passed out the exams, you couldn't resist making one last comment. As you placed the exam on my desk, you tightened your lips, shook your head, and stated with absolute assurance of the opposite, "I hope you pass." I snickered silently. *We'll see about that.*

With a self-assured gleam, you watched the class struggle with each question. You tapped rhythmically on the desk as if you were counting the beats to failure. As I placed my exam on your desk, you glared. I was the first one finished. Basking in my potential victory, I smiled sweetly and said, "See you tomorrow."

"Bring your crying towel," you called as I left the room.

A giant weight had been lifted from my shoulders, and I smiled for the entire drive home. I wanted to show you that in spite of your pushing, I could succeed.

The class was tense the next day. As you sat in the rolling chair behind your desk, you once again reminded everyone how difficult your tests were, and how anyone was fortunate to get a passing grade. I watched and waited.

Finally you stood, and I must admit, I swallowed hard.

But you performed magnificently, expounding the virtues of your high expectations as I sat, unmoving. You held a test paper high in the air and announced with great dramatic aplomb, "No one *ever* has gotten a 100 percent on one of my finals!"

Momentary shock set in as I was unsure if this was yet another sarcastic twist, but then I saw the infamous red ink with large exclamation points.

The class applauded and began laughing, and as the resolve showed on your face, you suddenly became a regular human being. You were speechless as you handed me my paper, and your smile and nodding acknowledgment remain clear in my memory. You didn't defeat me with your tough instruction, and I don't think either of us would have had it any other way.

I want to thank you, Dr. Maxis, for the experiences you provided. Thanks for helping me learn that no matter how bumpy the road becomes, or how many potholes there are, one can always rise above and be a success, no matter who is driving the vehicle.

YOUR FORMER PUNCHING-BAG A STUDENT
(WHO IS NOW MUCH WISER),

Dana Smith-Mansell
Pottsville, Pennsylvania

Dana Smith-Mansell holds a B.S. and a master's degree and is a published poet, writer, photographer, illustrator, and children's author residing in Pennsylvania. She is the author of Stop Bullying Bobby! Helping Children Cope with Teasing and Bullying.

The Living and the Dead

🍎 By Lois Courtenay Henderson 🍎

Dear Miss Reid,

As my biology teacher during my final years of schooling, you taught me as much about the living as you did about the dead. Perched high upon the four-legged stools that lined your laboratory benches at Sans Souci High School for Girls, in Newlands, Cape Town, you solicited our interest in the entrails of frogs and rats. Although excessively squeamish, as only a gaggle of teenage girls can be, we dutifully spread-eagled and dissected the latest range of newly killed specimens, painstakingly recording the details of their inner workings in our neatly kept notebooks.

Later, we positively glowed when you displayed our best efforts on parents' day to groups of gawking adults who, in some cases, could not believe the meticulous detail shown by their characteristically study-shy daughters.

Noting my solitary status as the youngest child of a divorced professional, you appeared to take a more than usual interest in my own welfare. Living in an apartment block across the road from us, you would drop by whenever you needed to collect botanical samples from Rondebosch Common, a large stretch of open land about eight minutes distant. You instilled pride in my ability to discern the finest examples you used to illustrate the topics of your upcoming classes—or at least that is what you emphatically led me to believe.

I still hold as one of my dearest memories of school-going days, winning the blessed prize of two carefully chosen books for coming in first in biology during my final year.

Hailing from an overtly religious background in which your parents featured largely as missionaries in the field, you epitomized the standard view of what, in adult life, we all expect Sunday school teachers to be—neat, prim, and self-contained.

In the eyes of zealously fashion-conscious teenagers coming from moderately wealthy homes, though, you appeared frumpish. Yet you radiated a sense of gentle goodness that served to transcend any such minor personal failings. I was delighted to hear, in my first year out of school, that you had accepted a proposal of marriage from the head of a private school. You, however, will always remain in my memory as Miss Reid, the teacher who really cared.

It was through your guidance that I also learned about the living Lord. Being unable to afford the cost of more exciting adventure camps that some of the other girls went on, there were Scripture Union camps held during the school holidays, which you encouraged me to attend. Gathering around the campfire or in crowded marquees in more inclement weather, I learned about a wiser and kinder Father than my own had been. In this way, I came to know more of the spirit that infused your own work and dedication to your profession—a spirit that I appreciate all the more as I approach my own more senior years.

More than thirty years later, I look back on the time that I spent with you as containing some of my most valued school experiences. Thank you, Miss Reid.

IN FOND AND HEARTFELT REMEMBRANCE,

Lois Courtenay Henderson
Velddrift, Western Cape, South Africa

Lois Courtenay Henderson is a retired librarian and teacher who lives in Velddrift, a small fishing village on the West Coast of South Africa. She edits dissertations and case studies for the University of Stellenbosch and compiles indexes for Maskew Miller Longman, a Cape Town publisher.

The Symmetry of Praise
🍎 By Kathy L. Reed 🍎

Dear Mrs. Parr,

I was the quiet girl in your sixth-grade class at Highlands Elementary in Huntsville, Alabama. It was easy not to notice me, as I worried so much about pleasing you that I would never have acted out. I was so insecure that I never even called attention to myself with other students.

That was 1968. My parents divorced that year, and both had remarried four months later. At that time, divorce was not as common as it is now, and I was very embarrassed to tell anyone about it. I was also having a hard time adjusting to my mom's new life, my stepdad, and my feeling of being invisible both at home and at school.

But teachers notice the things others miss, and you noticed me. Maybe it was the way I slumped in my chair or the weight I'd gained that year, or perhaps it was that I stopped caring about my hair being clean or my clothes being pressed. Or maybe you just noticed that I was crying out for help in my own silent way.

One afternoon as school was ending, you asked if I could stay for a few minutes to help you with a special project. You wanted to set up a reading corner, and asked if I would like to help choose the books. I loved books—devoured them, cherished them—but had very few of my own. You let me take home catalogs, and I sat in my room that night looking at all the books and reading the descriptions. You gave me the opportunity to choose those books and to read them, but more than that, you spent time with me.

Every day you asked how I was, and you praised me when I felt nothing I did mattered, and all the while, you continued to think of special projects I could do for you. I became closer to you than to my own mother, and I idolized you. I wanted to be just like you when I grew up. I wanted to wear my hair short and curled under like yours, to wear those skirt suits you wore, to stand tall like you when you said the Pledge of Allegiance.

The day I saw you cry when it was announced over the loudspeaker that Martin Luther King had been killed taught me more about love than anything I've ever experienced before or since. You were a white woman in the South in the '60s, and you recognized the value of the contribution Reverend King made.

Later that night, when I spoke to my parents about what had happened, the prejudice they carried came through in their comments. I knew they were wrong, because you didn't feel that way. Your view stayed with me throughout my life and made me want to be more caring about other races than my parents had been.

You gave me a role model for the kind of person I wanted to be, and influenced my life more than you will ever know. I am the woman I am today because you were my teacher.

THANK YOU, MRS. PARR.
I'LL ALWAYS LOVE YOU.
LOVE,

Kathy
Decatur, Alabama

Kathy L. Reed is a mother of four who lives in Decatur, Alabama, with her husband, Bruce. She has published several short stories and loves writing, travel, and playing the mountain dulcimer. www.writingsbykathy.com

Wild Blue Yonder

🍎 By Lisa M. Bolt Simons 🍎

Dear Mrs. Beverage,

It was September 1976. My mother, brother, and I had just moved to Colorado from Las Vegas, Nevada, almost four years after my dad was killed in a plane crash. On a Monday a few weeks after the school year began, I started second grade at Rockrimmon Elementary. That's when I met you.

Rockrimmon had so many students that fall of 1976 that portable trailers had been erected on campus to handle the overflow. I walked into one of these trailers as a new student, but I remember that day as if I were still there. Even now, I imagine watching a scared little girl entering class for the first time, holding her mother's hand. The door was open wide, and sunlight silhouetted the pair as they stepped into the room. The girl looked around at her new classmates' faces as she stood just behind her mother. She did not want her mom to leave her sight. Tears clouded her eyes when they said good-bye.

I was indeed that little girl, and you, Mrs. Beverage, approached me, bade goodbye to my mother, and guided me to my new desk. You looked a bit like Mrs. Brady from *The Brady Bunch*—your straight blond hair followed the curve of your head and curled up at the edges just above your shoulders. You were so friendly and made such an impression that I still remember you even as my own children start second grade almost thirty years later.

You introduced me to my new classmates, and then I had to stand in front of the students, tell them my name, and talk about my family and where we came from. I told my new classmates about my dad, who had attended and graduated from the Air Force Academy. I told how he became a USAF Thunderbird pilot, and that he died four years before. Despite my soft voice and shy demeanor, I remember that I was proud of my dad and his accomplishments. I told them of the dedication of a new building at Nellis Air Force Base named after him—Bolt Building—and the ceremony that would be held that coming December.

That day in September 1976, my first day of second grade in your class, I spoke about my dad and shared him with others for the first time. It seems the trauma of starting a new school planted the memory of my dad's death deeper than the years between age three and a half and seven. But things are the same in one respect: What my memory told me as a second grader—my father died and I knew him really only through photographs—is what my memory tells me today. But perhaps my second-grader mind held more recollection of a father lost just four years before, rather than the thirty-plus years after the fact.

Later that day, I was approached by a classmate named Mindy. She had thick, haylike hair and wore Coke-bottle glasses. She looked at me and said, "So what do they do at Bolt Building, make nuts and bolts out of your dad?"

I tattled to you, Mrs. Beverage, crying as I spoke.

I remember holding your hand as I stood by your side, tears falling without reserve as you told Mindy to apologize. It's a memory like a living memorial, one I remember much more clearly than the man of whom it speaks.

I will never forget you, Mrs. Beverage, and I want to thank you for helping a scared little girl bear the brunt of such a mean comment, and of such loss. In my mind I can still see you reprimanding Mindy and sending her back to her seat, and then you looking down at me, smiling, caring, encouraging, allowing me to cling to your side.

MOST SINCERELY,

Lisa M. Bolt Simons

Faribault, Minnesota

Lisa M. Bolt Simons is a writer and a teacher. She is working on her biggest project to date, her memoir entitled The Missing Man: A Daughter's Search for a Lost Thunderbird Pilot.

3. You Believed in Me

The human mind is a fascinating study. Capable of processing amazing amounts of information, it is in constant motion, always spinning with a deluge of new and exciting thoughts, creative endeavors, hopes, dreams, humorous experiences, and personal triumph and tragedy. Belief in one's own thoughts and convictions is commensurate with the amount of support and encouragement one receives when tackling everything from the simplest procedures to highly complex issues.

When dealing with such individual and diverse entities, the need for compassion is paramount, and teachers are some of the most compassionate individuals among us. Some carry themselves with the grace and valor of saints, while others provide insight on a more physical level, akin to a farmer tilling his field. What they all have in common, whether their methods are subtle or direct, is the amazing ability to show us, with unwavering loyalty, that we can do anything if we believe in ourselves.

Teachers give themselves to us mind, body, and soul. With each student, they revisit their life experiences and the experiences of everyone under their watchful eye. They are a wellspring of encouragement and insight and they tap into their own reserves on a daily basis in order that we may go forth in life to achieve our utmost potential. Teachers are astounding, the conduits for our psyches, and for that, many of us are eternally grateful.

The Three Musketeers

🍎 BY CHARLES W. ARNETT 🍎

Dear Mrs. Rich,

You must have known back in 1947 that we three
veterans, sitting together in the front row in English
101, liked you and enjoyed your classes. All these years
later, I would like to express again the depths of my
gratitude, and thank you for your influence on us and
our further achievements.

Already in our mid-to-late twenties, we were older
than the average student. We had served in World
War II and were just starting college on the GI Bill.
Paul served in the Intelligence Corps; Cliff was in
the infantry, where he received a Purple Heart and
disability compensation; and I had faced the blazing
guns of German ME-109s that disabled two of my
B-24 engines and damaged a third. After I crash-
landed in Nazi-occupied Holland, I survived nearly
a year of fatigue, hunger, and filth as a POW in
Germany.

We'd been called brave men—even heroes—but
the thought of having to take a college English class
terrified each of us.

Paul, a country boy from Montana, had never
stopped learning, even though he left school after
seventh grade to ride the rodeo circuit. When the GI
Bill passed, he applied to universities all around the
country, but since he lacked a high school diploma,
only Brigham Young University accepted him. He was

conscientious and determined but said he was scared spitless. Failing English could wash him out of BYU, and then where else could he turn? His very academic life might hang on passing English 101.

Cliff, an enthusiastic farm boy from Utah, admitted he was never much of a student in English classes. I had the same problem. Though at least average in high school, I found I knew almost nothing of what I ought to know about English.

Our trepidation increased at freshman orientation, when we were assigned to read the first hundred pages in a literary anthology before class even started! I shuddered at the thought of reading that much. Having barely glanced at the assignment, I really worried. Yet, I headed for the front seats. It was there that I first met Paul and Cliff, and we shared our anxiety.

Soon you entered the classroom and welcomed us. Your warm smile somehow quelled all our fears. As the lesson progressed, we discovered that you were actually interesting, and your reading assignments seemed manageable. After class, you approached us.

"You're my Three Musketeers," you said. "I'll expect to see you right here in the front row in every class." You also assured us you would "see us through." And you did. We felt special, although I suspect you treated every student with the same warm respect. You infused us with confidence, not just that day, but every time we met. We never missed a class, sat right in front of you, and enjoyed your teachings.

New horizons continued to open, and English 101 soon became a favorite class. I still remember much of the literature, and to this day, whenever I hear or use the word *ubiquitous,* I think of you and your assignment to write a paper about the ubiquitous reddleman in Thomas Hardy's *The Return of the Native.* But the most important lesson you taught me, Mrs. Rich, is that with faith, optimism, and hard work, I could achieve any goal I set. Passing English was the first of many.

Your Three Musketeers managed to earn bachelor's degrees. Diligent and studious Paul even graduated *summa cum laude.* All three of us received fellowships for postgraduate study at prestigious universities. Paul and Cliff both earned doctoral degrees. I had also planned to continue, but the Korean War broke out the summer we graduated, and I quickly changed my goal when I was recalled into the Air Force. I even served a year in Vietnam, shortly before I retired as a Lt. Colonel.

I can't speak for Cliff or Paul, but I know my life would be much poorer had I not had a wonderful teacher who lovingly guided me through that crucial English 101, and turned my fear of failure into a love for the English language and literature.

Thank you from the depths of my heart.

SINCERELY,

Charles W. Arnett
Duncan, Arizona

Charles W. Arnett has been married to Anna for over sixty years, is father of four sons and three daughters, and his posterity is already more than seventy. He enjoys reading—especially Scripture and Gospel themes—and serves faithfully and willingly wherever possible.

Matters of the Heart

🍎 By Crystal Schall 🍎

Dear Mr. McCollum,

I will never forget the day we met. I was so scared when I arrived at the band hall that hot summer day at Ragland High School in Alabama. Opening the door, I had no idea what to expect. I was in tenth grade and felt I had a daunting task before me. I had a new band director and was debuting as sax section leader.

There were butterflies fluttering in my stomach, and I was afraid you would hear their frantic fight for freedom. Would I be able to handle the responsibility? What would the other kids think of me? Did I really have what it takes to be a leader?

You didn't even know me—only my reputation—but you put me at ease almost immediately. You believed I could do it . . . that I had what it takes. Somehow you instinctively knew that I was meant to lead, and that I could be trusted with responsibility. And because of you, I succeeded.

Whether concerns were mine or those of my fellow bandmates didn't matter, because you made me feel I could come to you with any issue, could face any challenge head-on, and ultimately persevere. From you I learned that the needs of the many outweigh the needs of the one. No one hears you; they hear the band.

You also taught me to always stand up for the little guy, not to cower down to anyone, to fight for what I believe, and to remember that no matter what you're doing, someone is always watching. As a result, I learned to be a strong woman who can not only take care of herself, but take care of those around her.

Homecoming of my junior year you chose a song that included a duet for trumpet and saxophone that I was to play. I had never performed in front of the band with that many people watching, and once again, I was terrified. So many things were going wrong, not the least of which was that all the members of the band could not be together at the same time to practice. You pulled me out of class and surprised us all by getting out your trumpet and accompanying me so I'd be ready for my big night. You gave me confidence when I could not find it within myself, and because of you, I know I can handle whatever life throws at me.

Tragically, we lost you later that year when you had to leave our school because your heart was giving out on you. A new band director was brought in, and though I was still section leader, I disliked the new guy because I thought he was trying to replace you. I gave him a hard time about everything because I knew in my heart that you would come back. After all, you had taught me never to run from a fight. All I needed to do was be patient—something I was never any good at.

You never got the heart you so badly needed, and it's no wonder. In order for a transplant to work, they have to find a heart the same size as the one it's replacing. I should have known they wouldn't find one, because there has never been a heart as big as yours. Every child you ever taught had a special place in your heart, and though I'm sure I never told you, you will always have a special place in mine.

WITH MUCH LOVE AND RESPECT,

Crystal Schall
Ragland, Alabama

Crystal Schall is a freelance writer. She lives in the southeastern United States, homeschooling three very special sons with the support of her loving husband, William.

Profile in Courage

By Arjean Spaite

Dear Mrs. Keir,

It was a gold-painted paper plate decorated with painted macaroni, and it served as a frame for a child's silhouette. A typical first-grade art project. I'm sure you forgot it long ago, but I will never forget.

To explain how much you mean to me, Mrs. Keir, I have to go back to my kindergarten year—a year that I would much rather forget. It was 1963 at E.J. Blott Elementary School, in Liberty Township, Ohio. My teacher was old, crabby, and ready to retire. I was shy, timid, and not very happy to be there.

The last straw for me came on a day in late fall. The weather had turned cold, and coats were a necessity. My parents took me shopping, and I was so proud of the beautiful jacket I picked out. It was a soft cream-colored fleece, with bright red, orange, and gold leaves scattered across it. It had a hood, zipped up the front, and to my little-girl eyes, it was the most gorgeous coat I had ever seen. I couldn't wait to wear it to school the next day!

Things went well that day until it was time to go home. We were all putting on our coats, and our teacher was walking around helping children and generally grousing. Suddenly, right before she got to me, she stopped. She was helping a disabled girl in our class zip up her coat, when she screamed, "If you can't zip your own coats, don't wear coats with zippers! I will not do this for you anymore!" Well, I couldn't zip my pretty new coat. I came home in tears, and my parents had to take me out that night and buy a different coat that I could fasten myself. I was devastated.

From that day on, kindergarten was a nightmare. My older brother dragged me onto the bus every morning, often with me still crying and begging my mom to let me stay home. I don't have a single pleasant memory of kindergarten, unless you count walking out the door the last day and knowing that I didn't have to go back.

Summer passed, and it was time to go to first grade. I wasn't happy, but I went, and you were my teacher. It was different from the start. You were young, enthusiastic, and you smiled all the time. I no longer dreaded going to school, but I was still very timid and shy, and honestly, I think I was waiting for things to go back to how they had been the year before. I just wasn't sure that going to school was the thing for me.

With parent-teacher conferences approaching, you had us do an art project for our parents to take home that night. We spray-painted paper plates and macaroni shells gold, then glued the shells around the outside of the plates like a frame. You spent an afternoon in front of an overhead projector, patiently tracing each of our silhouettes onto paper. You then shrunk them down and cut them out of black construction paper for us to glue onto our frames.

When all the silhouettes were done, you looked at the class, smiled, and said, "There is one more person who needs to be traced. I want my silhouette done as well. Who would like to trace me?" Hands waved wildly as the bold children in the class volunteered. I sat back quietly. I knew I would never be picked, and I knew I wasn't good enough to trace a beautiful teacher like you.

Then suddenly, you called my name. "Arjean, would you come and trace my silhouette?" I couldn't believe what I was hearing. I got up, and with shaking hands I did the tracing. When I was done, you smiled and told me I had done a perfect job. I was so proud and couldn't wait to go home and tell my parents that you had picked *me* to do such a special and important job.

It was a little thing, but it changed my attitude toward school. Suddenly, I loved getting up in the morning to go to school. I was still shy, but I started coming out of my shell. Because I felt that you believed in me, I began to believe in myself, and that attitude stayed with me through high school, college, and earning my professional certification.

A silly grade school art project? Perhaps, but it changed my school life and it changed me. Thank you for showing this child the light, and encouraging me to follow it.

SINCERELY,

Arjean Spaite
Boardman, Ohio

Arjean Spaite is a CPA who resides in Boardman, Ohio, with her husband, three teenage sons, and two dogs. She is a black belt in karate who enjoys reading and writing in her spare time.

It's All in the Delivery . . .

🍎 By Glenda Stovall Schoonmaker 🍎

Dear Professor Brown,

I'm sure you would not remember me. There was nothing significant about me, unless you consider my reputation outside the classroom. It was, after all, college years in the late 1960s, the era of free love and peace. Our official college motto was "Turn On." I'm not sure if any students related that to "Turn On" in terms of study, but I guess that's what it meant. For my part, studying or excelling academically wasn't exactly my focus.

I was a freshman at the University of Science and Arts of Oklahoma in Chickasha. My major was speech communication and drama, and I was in your Acting 1 class. I hardly remember any of the students or the assignments—except one particular exercise, and something you said.

We were studying ancient Greek plays and how tragedy was never shown onstage. As a result, you assigned each of us to do a Greek messenger scene. *Oh, brother! How ridiculous,* I thought. It was bad enough thinking about trotting onto the stage and gesturing passionately to announce the events, but to utter them in the language of the time of Euripides' plays?

"All hail! ye victors, maidens of Mycenae, to all Orestes' friends, his triumph I announce; Aegisthus, the murderer of

Agamemnon, lies weltering where he fell; return thanks to heaven."

I could just see me now, looking stupid through and through. And stupid is how I always felt. I tried to hide it. I tried to dress nicely. I tried to fit in. When I bothered to go to class or turn in assignments, I usually made good grades—sometimes even A's. But that was just a façade. I wasn't worth anything inside and I knew it.

But I did the assignment. I halfway memorized the lines and ran onto the stage shouting the tragic events that ensued on the battlefield. I did it. I felt stupid. I didn't care what grade I got because grades didn't matter. The assignment was done.

It's now almost forty years later, but your words still resonate in my ears:

"That's the worst piece of crap I've ever seen. I will not accept that. You are far more capable than that. You *will* do the assignment over tomorrow."

I was mortified. I was humiliated. I didn't care if I flunked the assignment!

The easiest thing for you to do would have been to give me an F, but you didn't. You didn't allow me to snivel out of the assignment. "You are more capable than that. Do it over," you said.

So, I memorized the lines, practiced my delivery, and presented the assignment the next day. I could feel the pleasure not only from you, as a teacher, but from me because I knew I had done my best. Those few words taught me to push myself past the easy road.

Professor Brown, I became a high school speech communication teacher and drama coach, and I've always remembered your class. You taught me that as teachers, we need to pull for the best from our students. I never let any students take a zero or an F because they didn't want to do an assignment.

Sometimes we need to see that someone else believes in us before we can believe in ourselves. I didn't believe in myself, but you did—even if it was only for one assignment. Because you wouldn't allow me to take the easy way out, you impacted my entire teaching career. Your one statement helped open my eyes to see past the façade of students whose shoulders shrug, "I don't care."

You helped me to start believing in myself, and in turn, I hope I've helped many other students believe in themselves. Thank you for something you didn't even know you did.

SINCERELY,

Glenda Schoonmaker
Lake Havasu City, Arizona

Glenda Stovall Schoonmaker is a freelance writer, speaker, and personality trainer. You can find out more about her at www.glendaschoonmaker.com.

You Are What You Read

By Arlene L. Mandell

Dear Mr. Halperin,

When I was thirteen and a sophomore at Franklin K. Lane, I had the good fortune to be assigned to your honors history class. I was a shy girl from a working-class family in the East New York section of Brooklyn. You were the assistant dean of students, a man who could make the toughest punk at Lane cringe and cower.

Although I was hoping to go to college, I was also taking stenography and typing so I would have a "useful" profession. In the spring of 1954, I had one free class period and became your secretary. I remember typing a letter three times. First you changed one word and I retyped it. Then you deleted a comma. Finally, you showed me what was really wrong—I was folding the paper in half and then into thirds to insert it in the business-sized envelope.

One day I must have mentioned to you that I had read *War and Peace* the previous summer. You seemed impressed, but I didn't tell you I'd skipped many pages, because I was more interested in the romances of Natasha Rostov than the descriptions of war.

You asked what newspaper I read. "*The Daily News*," I said. What else was there? Bold, racy headlines. Great sports stories, though by then, my once-beloved Brooklyn Dodgers were firmly entrenched in faraway Los Angeles. "This is what a young woman with your potential must read," you said, handing me your neatly folded copy of the *New York Times*.

At first I found the *Times* too detailed and boring, but soon I was reading at least a third of "All the News That's Fit to Print" and learning more than I could from any textbook. Then one day, you gave me *The New Yorker,* with its elegant drawings on the cover and the "Talk of the Town" section filled with chitchat about art gallery openings and famous writers and their peculiar habits. I sometimes imagined myself in these places, drinking cocktails and being witty.

During our brief chats, I learned your wife was a librarian at Columbia University, and that you had no children. I fantasized about being your daughter, imagining myself sitting between the two of you at Carnegie Hall or having lunch at Tavern on the Green— all the things I'd read about in Talk of the Town.

What I didn't realize then, Mr. Halperin, was that I was on my way out of working-class Brooklyn, and you were providing me with the road map. When my parents couldn't afford to send me to college, you talked to the guidance counselor and found a job for me at New York University, where I could work as a secretary during the day and take eight free credits each term at night.

Do you remember the time we met for lunch? It was a few months after I started my new life as a secretary/college student. We met at a little Spanish restaurant in Greenwich Village. I told you about my economics professor, who threw things—paper airplanes, pencils, once even a book—at students who weren't paying attention. You confided to me that your wife had breast cancer.

Years later, I tried to locate you to tell you about my first small successes as a writer, but by then you had retired from Franklin K. Lane, and the phone company no longer had a New York listing for you.

I know I've never properly thanked you for all your guidance. Even now, a half century later and a long way from Brooklyn, I read the *New York Times* every morning. And whenever I send a letter to an editor with a poem or an essay, I fold the paper properly.

YOUR GRATEFUL STUDENT,

Arlene
Santa Rosa, California

Arlene L. Mandell, formerly Arlene Kostick, Franklin K. Lane Class of '57, is a retired English professor now living in Santa Rosa, California.

Emerging from the Shadows
🍎 By Joan Hobernicht 🍎

Dear Mrs. Reber,

I recently had occasion to sort through over seventy-three years of lifetime accumulations and found a black-and-white photo of myself you took in 1939. I was in the second grade, and you were my teacher.

There I was, grinning from ear to ear outside the pink-stuccoed one-room rural schoolhouse, proudly clutching a framed painting in front of me. I wore a cotton print dress with ties in the back, and my Buster Brown haircut sported a matching ribbon tied in a bow. My feet were encased in white anklets and black patent-leather shoes.

The painting was my prize for winning first place in the Meade County Declamatory Contest in my division, and I was so proud. Finally, I could do something my two older sisters couldn't do. They could sing, dance, draw pictures, and get A's on their report cards, but public speaking left them terrified.

You were an excellent teacher. I thought you were beautiful. You wore attractive clothing, and your brown hair shone in the upswept hairstyle of the time. Young and dedicated, you intuitively sought to discover my hidden talent as I languished in the shadows of my overachieving sisters.

Your patience was never ending as I strove to memorize my "piece." Gentle suggestions improved my delivery, and when I practiced in front of the class, you sternly stared down the snickers and laughter of my siblings.

My mother thanked you for your effort on my behalf. "Maybe my ugly duckling will turn into a swan someday," she said.

My picture and story were featured in the local weekly paper. I had my fifteen minutes of fame at the tender age of seven.

I was brokenhearted when you left our school after two years and chose to teach in town so you wouldn't have to drive so far. We lost touch as you and your military husband moved from one exotic place to another. I wonder if you ever thought of me. Did you know what a wonderful influence you had on me? I'm sure I was not the only one to benefit from your expertise and innate kindness.

I heard that you never had children of your own and were eventually divorced. You continued to teach and therefore better the lives of countless children. If you are still living, you are in your nineties. Are you still active in children's education? I'm sure you are if you are able.

How I would love to sit by your side and relive those days of my awakening. Time has not erased the gratitude I feel for you. I confess I don't know what happened to the painting I received on that occasion. I would rather have had a doll, but even at that age, I knew it was not the gift, but the significance of it.

Everyone has a talent of some kind hidden in the dark recesses of their mind. Sometimes it takes a caring person to open the door and gently coax it out. Thank you again, Mrs. Reber.

GRATEFULLY YOURS,

Joan Hobernicht,
née Inga Joan Speakman
Lake Havasu City, Arizona

Joan Hobernicht was born in South Dakota and attended and taught in rural schools there. She is a retired married mother of four and grandmother of ten, who enjoys writing novels, essays, and children's stories.

The Miracle Worker

🍎 BY ELAINE GREEN 🍎

Dear Mrs. Draper,

Even though you taught me fifth-grade English
at Alfred J. Lawless Elementary in New Orleans,
the greatest lessons I learned from you had little, if
anything, to do with language. You were the only
teacher I knew who had the amazing ability to teach
even when you weren't saying a word.

If you were with another adult when I approached,
you'd stoop down and look fully into my eyes while I
spoke. Your very demeanor announced that—for the
moment—I was the center of your universe. At the
time, it seemed yours were the only eyes in the world
that were fixed on me. They danced when I excelled
and showed concern when I fell short. You'd glance a
certain way, and I would stop bullying or disrupting
your class. Once, I even saw you brush a tear away
when I aced my Keats recitation. That told me that my
success was important to you—that I mattered to you.
I needed eyes then, and yours were always there.

I also grew to love your ears, especially when you
cupped them in my direction. I studied my verbs more
carefully to make sure I used the proper tenses, because
I knew you were listening. I curbed my bad language
because I didn't want to offend you. If I was babbling
about something about which I had little knowledge,

you listened even then. I felt empowered to achieve because I owned Mrs. Draper's ears.

How easily you worked miracles without words. With a simple wave of your hand, you could make the whole class pipe down and listen because "Elaine" had the floor. That really made me feel special.

At home, my mother's ears were often too distracted by my baby sister's crying—too turned off, I guess, from my dad's complaints. And in a world of false friends, it was wonderful to find a haven where I could hide and be heard. I needed ears then, and you lent me yours.

Finally, I loved you because you were the "rottenest" teacher in the world. Our class often played a silly game while coming in from recess. Do you remember, "Last one in is a rotten egg?" I was the selfish one who pushed and bullied any poor sucker who lagged last, and tripped anyone who dared get in my way.

One day I didn't move fast enough, and it was clear that for the first time, I'd be coming in last. Without a word, you scooted to the end of the line behind me to make sure I wasn't the rotten egg that day. *"Wow!"* I thought. *"Who would do that?"*

That was a special day for me. That day, I learned the importance of putting other people's feelings ahead of my own. I understood what it means to walk in the other person's shoes, and that showing is better than telling.

This letter is many years overdue. It comes to say thanks for being both eyes and ears to a kid who was floundering and careening out of control.

That moment you stood in my place—like Patty Duke in *The Miracle Worker*—my senses sprang alive, and I found my place in the world. On that day, Mrs. Draper, you showed one rotten kid what love can do. Thanks for working that miracle in me.

SINCERELY,

Elaine Green
New Orleans, Louisiana

Elaine Green is a freelance writer, avid reader, and native New Orleanian.

More Than Music

🍎 By Julia Petre 🍎

Dear Mr. Stevens,

Two years ago, I sat in your band room wringing my hands around the barrel of my plastic clarinet, wearing overly large clothes and glasses. My hair was in a braid and I tugged on the loose curls every few minutes, trying to calm myself.

I imagined myself flubbing the notes under the pressure, and hearing you tell me I didn't make "top band." That I would be the first in my family not to make the cut as a freshman. That I was as worthless as my private teacher told me I was.

I felt my throat tighten when I overheard you telling the tuba player before me that he needed a year in the lower band, and I took a sip of water, telling myself to stop shaking. I held on to the cheap plastic as my entire body trembled.

You called my name. I told myself I could prove everyone wrong, but I didn't believe it. Under my breath, I muttered, "Whatever you do, don't cry, Julia. Don't cry."

As I was about to play, you asked, "Are you nervous?" I nodded, too petrified to speak. "Julia, you have no right to be nervous! I'm the one who should be nervous. If you play this piece perfectly, I'll have nothing to teach you and they'll fire me."

I tried not to giggle.

The rest of the audition went by in a blur. You ushered me into your office, and while I stared at the strange decorations, you talked about the responsibilities of being in marching band. I had done it. I had proved them all wrong!

At the start of the next school year, I walked into the same band room, carrying my cheap plastic clarinet and a hat. I also brought the memory of my private teacher telling me after the earlier audition that I didn't deserve to make the band. I believed him.

You handed me the music and smiled, but I felt a surge of guilt. When the band played together, I barely made a sound, instead trying to hide. I didn't belong with these amazing musicians.

Then I played a wrong note and everyone heard.

I imagined them deciding how to kick me out. At lunch, afraid, I spoke to no one. After lunch, you pulled the freshmen aside—myself included—and told us that you wanted us to be there. You reached out to all of us and accepted us. But still I felt unworthy.

Weeks later, in my private lesson, I waited for my teacher to help me work on my competition piece. A tiny man with a thick mustache, he sat down and asked for a scale. I froze, messed up three times, and felt my heart sink. He told me never to come back—I was worthless.

The next morning, I went to your band class. Holding back tears, I plopped down on the couch in your office and told you the truth. I told you how I didn't measure up. How I wasn't good enough.

You told me that I was wrong and that you'd chosen me for a reason. That you saw potential in me. On a little slip of white paper, you wrote down the name and phone number of a new teacher—someone who would never throw me out.

Over the next year I worked hard, refusing to let a mistake exist. I still hid from the world, playing only with my bedroom door closed, but when I returned the following fall, carrying the same cheap plastic clarinet and a new hat, I found myself playing first part, and playing the right notes. I stood out, but now because I did something well. As a result, you invited me to join full orchestra, to play second clarinet, and to play solos!

During a performance, as the orchestra finished its second piece, the audience applauded, and we stood up. The other clarinetist left the stage, leaving me with a solo. You were on your feet, applauding. I saw you cheering me on.

I took a breath and began to play, my hands shaking as I tried to give each note life. With the orchestra backing me, the sound of my clarinet soared over the audience, keeping them silent. I stood up, the soloist, to the applause of my bandmates in the audience. You gave me the confidence to believe in myself.

This year, when I return with a wooden clarinet and yet another new hat, I will be a part of the band, and a featured soloist in orchestra. Thank you, Mr. Stevens.

SINCERELY,

Julia Petre

Clarksville, Maryland

Julia Petre is a sixteen-year-old who attends Atholton High School in Columbia, Maryland. She plans to major in creative writing in college.

The Strength of Soft Words

🍎 By A. G. Dammer 🍎

Dear Mrs. Patillo,

In 1981, I was in the twelfth grade at Dulaney High School in Timonium, Maryland, and I still remember exactly where you lived at the time, because you so generously shared your home for meetings of the group you mentored, Future Business Leaders of America.

Back in that era, our neighborhood was mostly white, and you walked among us with your spine straight, with beauty, and with grace. By being exactly who you are, by bringing us into your home, and by bringing your husband to attend our many class celebrations, you invited us to truly know you. And you cared enough to truly know me.

During that time, my father had died, and my mom had remarried. Alcohol flowed through our home—and bulimia had become my dieting tool. You had the courage to bring my bulimia out into the open as you faced my parents' wrath and embarrassment. In doing so, you removed the cloak of secrecy I needed to continue my compulsion. In doing so, you saved my life.

I remember when you told me your husband was impressed by me—by my smile. He said I was the only one he really noticed smiling at your Christmas party. Still grieving from my losses, I didn't even realize I'd been smiling.

You taught me how easy and how powerful a smile can be, and even though I know others must have smiled too, for a seventeen-year-old with a bulimic self-image, his comment about me was a pivotal moment.

By the spring of that school year, you'd pushed me to compete in Parliamentary Procedure, and I didn't want to let you down. It still makes me smile that I forgot crucial names in the final competition, and that you never mentioned that my lapses put us in last place. I never was good with names. Maybe you knew that, too.

Remember how you taught us to use only black bobby pins for our graduation caps? Remember when you taught us to scuff the bottoms of our new shoes before wearing them across the stage so we wouldn't slip on camera? Details were always important to you, but to you, we were always more than details.

Today I'm blessed to be the "minority" on a North Carolina college campus. I am blessed to teach remedial courses that help adults go to college—no matter what they experienced in high school. Many are my age or older and back in school for the first time in decades. I have so much in common with so many— from high school horrors and early family difficulties to building and nurturing our own families.

A smile is still my most useful tool, and I follow your example of soft words and strong spirit. And so often, as in your classroom, I am blessed with friendship and love.

**GOD BLESS YOU, MRS. PATILLO.
AND THANK YOU.**

Annette Dammer
Dunn, North Carolina

A. G. Dammer is a homeschooling mom, wife, college English instructor, ex-journalist, and founder of www.writershelper. org *and* Teenlight *magazine (www.teenlight.org). She wrote* Ready, Set, Go! *(Baker Books, 2003) and is currently completing* The Cat Chased the Rat: An Aggie Panther Mystery.

Making the Cut

By William Cassius Ruthardt Divney

Dear Jon Lispsky,

When I first entered Boston University as an undergraduate in theater, I was loaded with confidence and enthusiasm. I knew I was entering one of the finest theater schools in the country. I couldn't have guessed what was in store for me, and how my spirit would be shot down before I could truly shine.

From day one I had a big red target on my back. I was excited and completely naive. There were fifty-nine fresh faces in the program, and I made friends fast, but there was no room for complacency. I had some major growing to do, and you, Jon, were the driving force behind me, scaring me into becoming a man. At the time I really resented you. Perhaps you found me peculiar because I was eccentric, but in retrospect, you were trying to champion me. It was all about "tough" love, and that's exactly what I needed at the time.

We started out with a class of sixty people. Over the course of two years, half our class was cut, and other people simply got fed up and left. Emotions ran high, and we would find out whether or not we were worthy of return to the acting program by reading a letter tacked up on a board at the end of the year. I can remember the devastation coloring the faces of some of my dearest friends as they read their rejection letters, tears streaming down.

During our biannual conferences, with five professors and the chairman of the program, certain professors would make inane judgments about various students. Some people were told that they were too overweight, had limited acting range, or were too "quirky." We were essentially bombarded with all kinds of warnings. Yes, the *dreaded warning*. Oftentimes, professors openly disagreed, and this caused even more confusion. As it turned out, I was one of the students caught in limbo. Certain acting professors were rallying support for me, while others would make guarded remarks. "You'll only do commercial work," one said.

And then you stepped up.

"You slip and slide with your socks on the floor in class, and it makes you look young," you said.

You told me I needed to make a 180-degree turn. I needed to play characters who were strong—characters with conviction. Admittedly, I was a late bloomer. I looked fifteen, and nobody knew what to do with me. I was a softy, not a fighter. But that soon changed.

Fear is what inspired me, and proving to you that I was capable of rising to any challenge was my goal. As a result, I was motivated to study abroad and take a second major at the school of communications—no easy task, considering how much work and time were involved. My class advisor, Sidney Friedman, looked into my eyes and called me "Willful William." He knew I could do it, just as you did. Conviction was now part of my repertoire.

A young directing student from Australia quickly gravitated toward me and gave me leading roles in all of his shows. He even went as far as casting me as a woman. You later told me that I was one of the funniest and "emotionally available" people that you knew. You passed me into the second year, and without your green light, I would have been gone.

At the end of my first semester of junior year, I had the best conference of my college career. I felt like I was winning an Academy Award for best actor. However, I was emotionally exhausted. I missed my friends who were long gone, and I needed a change. So, with my conviction intact, I decided to take a year off to broaden my horizons.

After all was said and done, I *was* cut from the program—but by my own choice. I walked out of that room with all of my dignity and a little bit from those who'd already fallen.

I have you to thank for helping me face my fears, Jon, and for instilling in me the confidence to make difficult choices.

BEST REGARDS,

William Cassius Divney
New York, New York

William Cassius Ruthardt Divney graduated from Performing Arts High School in New York and holds theater arts and public relations degrees from Boston University. A graduate student at Columbia University, he is a director, actor, and animal activist. He dedicates this letter to Felicia Shpall (1970–2005), childhood friend and college peer.

The Madness of Eccentricity
🍎 By Barb Karg 🍎

Dear Jack,

It's been a decade since we met for lunch, and a decade before that since I drove off the University of California, Davis, grounds and into the big bad world. Though you've no doubt seen hundreds of writers come and go, you'll be happy to know I'm still standing, still writing, and still maintaining a sense of humor.

I can honestly say that never a day goes by when I don't benefit from the wisdom and humor of your teachings, and it seems only right that you should know how much you are appreciated.

Though attending university was always my goal, I never felt completely in tune with the educational world. One often finds that there are two schools of thought, one for those individuals who benefit from the principles and practices of a classical education, and one for those who benefit from the wisdom of the streets by learning through life experiences. I fall into the latter category. Which is not to say I was a poor student, I was just a lousy test taker who bored easily.

I've always admired you. You had the patience of a saint, and the rare gifts required to help everyone recognize their own quirky talents. In my case, you offered me a challenge, and though I may not have been aware of it at the time, the message was clear. The results of our time together helped me to think and write and live my life straight from the heart.

The first day I walked into your creative fiction writing class was the first time in my schooling that I knew I was in the right place. You were always careful to balance your commentary, especially when you were just getting to know a writer. Balance, and the ability to see all sides of a story, is second nature to me now. I learned that from you.

As the years progressed, and as my advisor and friend, you and I spent many classes wrestling through storylines and assignments, familiarity allowing us to speak freely about everything from Truman Capote to taco sauce.

What you don't know is that you helped me realize something that for years had vexed my mortal soul, and it had more to do with my eccentric thought process than it did my writing style.

One of the last classes we had together was American literature. It was a large class in a small theater. I'd always despised large classrooms. I'd never dare utter a word, but this time was different, so I started to ask questions and contribute thoughts when the room grew still. Subsequently, if I looked like I was hiding behind a tall guy, you'd hunt me down and pose some scenario, forcing me to quickly ramble something off. But on one particular day, you asked a specific question and I answered by making a bizarre analogy to the story of *Little Red Riding Hood*.

"*Little Red Riding Hood*? Where did that come from?" you raved, as all eyes turned to the back of the room. "How in God's name are you making that connection? It has absolutely nothing to do with the theme and was certainly not the writer's intent. What are you thinking?"

Needless to say, I remained silent for the rest of the hour. After class, I ran you down as you attempted to escape to your office.

"What was that all about?" I asked. "That was a perfectly legitimate observation, and an entirely new way of looking at an overanalyzed piece of work."

"Yes it was," you said calmly.

"Huh?" I was vexed.

"That was a brilliant leap and it made perfect sense."

Consternation.

"Then why did you lay into me?" I said.

"Because I didn't think of it first."

There it was, and to this day, it makes me laugh. I doubt you even recall the incident, but it wasn't until that very moment that I came to realize that the difference between a good writer and an exceptional writer is being able to think outside the box.

Recognizing that you have the ability to break out of a circle of stagnant thought is a battle worth fighting. I have you to thank for that epiphany, and for all the wonderful hours spent learning what it is to translate what one sees, hears, and observes into colorful prose that one hopes will touch the hearts and minds of all who read it.

Couldn't have done it without you, Jack.

YOU'RE ALWAYS IN MY THOUGHTS,

Barb

The Oregon Coast

Barb Karg is a veteran journalist, author, graphic designer, and screenwriter. She resides in the Pacific Northwest with her better half, Rick, and five four-legged children. At any given time, they all drive her nuts.

4. You Inspired Me

The beauty of true inspiration, especially if it comes in the form of an individual, is a constant source of strength. At their very core, teachers are inspired individuals. They arise each day with the purpose of educating minds both young and mature in ways that are not always self-evident. Their cause is noble and their goal pure as they touch the hearts of all those who seek their counsel and compassionate guidance.

To be truly inspired and to make something of the energy that comes with such a gift is to be truly fulfilled. Teachers share with us the wonders of the world, the art of science, the beauty of words, and the soul inherent in all living things. Inspiration solicits movement, creativity, thought, and action. To inspire is to promote the best aspect of living, and individuals who teach bring knowledge and excitement to all they encounter, allowing us to blend into the landscape of our hearts and minds.

Old Crow

🍎 By Mary Cook 🍎

Dear Mr. Crowley-Smith,

The Victorian school building stood out like a decaying tooth in the mouth of hell, surrounded as it was by the desolation of postwar Britain. Bomb sites were our play areas, but you were the dashing war hero who would lead me beyond the ruins.

Even your name, "double-barreled" as we called it, sounded aristocratic and hinted at a world beyond the one I'd been brought into.

Arundel Street Junior Mixed School was in the center of Portsmouth on the south coast of England. A major naval port, the city had lost about one third of its homes and business premises to German bombs.

I was proud to have you as my class teacher. A man of many passions, you had a talent to convey them to others. No dry academic, you lived and breathed whatever subject you were teaching at any particular time.

An ex–fighter pilot, you'd been shot down three times by enemy fire. I was going to marry you when I grew up. The fact that you were already married, with five children, meant nothing to my eight-year-old mind. Coy about my crush, I referred to you privately as "Old Crow."

Thoroughly steeped in the arts, you were an ardent admirer of Vincent van Gogh. One day, you brought in a reproduction of the artist's *Sunflowers*, and we painted

sunflowers that looked like blobs of yellow paint.
But then you told us the story of how van Gogh had
gone mad and cut off part of his ear—stirring stuff for
first-year juniors. After that, we felt inspired to paint
sunflowers with fresh vigor.

Another day, you collected fistfuls of bluebells, and
we streaked our paper with the searing purple-blues we
found in our pastel tins.

You taught me to see.

One day I was working on a painting of a building
using gray-white tints for the windows. It was the
childish means I used to express transparency. You
promptly lifted me onto a desk so that I could look at
the windows of the classrooms opposite.

"What color do they appear to you?" you asked.

"They look almost black to me, sir," I reported.

"Almost black," you agreed.

Taking up my brush again, I painted "almost
black" windows.

Another of your passions was archaeology. One
day you came into class carrying a brown paper bag
containing numerous fragments of Roman pottery.
When you asked who would like a piece to keep,
thirty-plus hands shot toward the ceiling.

You then walked around the room, placing a
pottery shard on each desk. I handled my fragment
reverently, out of respect for the toga-clad individual
whose long-dead fingers had created the pot and
decorated it with cross-hatching. That day, we made
Roman-style pots from modeling clay.

You loved poetry and drama. A talented actor, you were the leading light in the Southsea Shakespeare Actors. You introduced us to the traditional poetry of the border ballads. My favorite was "Lord Randall," with its story of a young nobleman poisoned by his sweetheart. I particularly enjoyed intoning the chilling refrain:

"Mother, make my bed soon, for I'm weary wi' hunting and fain would lie doon. . . ."

You were critical of those of us who wasted time at the cinema, but thoroughly approved of the radio—the "wireless," as it was known then. I remember you sternly rebuking a boy who pronounced it "woiless."

In those days, the way one spoke mattered. If you let it be known you came from a poor background, you stayed poor. I was deeply offended when you thought I had adenoids, when it was just the perpetual cold suffered by all children in my district. But you raised our sights by giving us the social advantages that came with elocution lessons.

In the unlikely event of your still being alive, you'd be proud to know that somewhere, there's a moderately successful writer who was one of your "mixed juniors." I'd like to thank you for your valuable lessons in living.

YOURS TRULY,

Mary Cook née *Stinton*
Alford, Lincolnshire, England

Mary Cook is a UK-based freelance writer and former newspaper reporter. Her articles, poems, and short stories have appeared in numerous publications, both in print and online.

You Proved Me Wrong

🍎 By Vanessa A. Romanko 🍎

Dear Señora Ober,

On the first day of Spanish class, you read us a paragraph in a language that we knew nothing about, and I didn't understand a word of it. From the panicked faces I saw around the room, none of my classmates did either. You promised us that on the last day of class when you reread it, we would understand. I rolled my eyes, knowing that there was no way I would be able to comprehend something so foreign by June. I gave you 180 days to prove me wrong, but remained content in knowing that you wouldn't be able to do it.

It was 1996, and my freshman year at Spotswood High School in Spotswood, New Jersey, flew by. Your Spanish class quickly became my most atypical, not to mention my favorite, class. You taught us through arts and crafts, music, and pictures. All of your classes were incredibly visually stimulating. You opened my eyes to a new way of learning by seeing. Your lessons were always fun, and just unusual enough to be completely memorable. Before I knew it, I found myself looking forward to your class the last period of the day.

I was having such a good time learning that by June, I barely realized that the 180th day had arrived. I had done well throughout the year, and felt that I had learned a reasonable amount of new information (as well as developed quite a taste for Spanish *Chupa*

Chups lollipops), but that certainly didn't mean that I understood Spanish. You still had to prove me wrong, as you'd promised so many months ago.

I walked into your class for the last time, ever skeptical, and listened as you reread the passage from the first day of school. My jaw dropped in amazement when, as promised, I understood every word! All of those episodes of *Muzzy* cartoons and silly mnemonic devices had actually come together to form something surprisingly intelligible. I looked around at the rest of the class. The stunned faces that surrounded me proved that everyone else had also understood. The feeling of pride and accomplishment that came over me was incredible, and it is something that I will never forget.

Looking back as an adult, I can see that you gave me the confidence I needed for success in learning all levels of Spanish. You are genuinely the best teacher I've ever had. It can't be easy to teach a room full of novices a completely new language, yet you were able to do it in a way that remains fresh in my mind nearly a decade later.

I owe much of my success in Spanish to you and the confidence that you gave me throughout my freshman year. Remembering the remarkable feeling of accomplishment I had on the last day of your class is something that motivates me to continue learning Spanish.

I have the utmost respect for good language teachers, and you are truly a great one. Thank you, Señora Ober, for helping me gain the confidence that could only have come from the ability to understand. I hope you enjoyed proving me wrong.

MIL GRACIAS,

Vanessa (Sofía)
Milltown, New Jersey

A resident of New Jersey, Vanessa A. Romanko holds a bachelor's degree in business administration from Rowan University. She is going back to school to pursue a career as a Spanish teacher.

Triple-Whammy

🍎 By Paula Munier 🍎

Dear Sister Esther,

It's been more than thirty years since we met, so this thank-you comes a little late. But only now as I grow older and look back on my life do I truly understand how rich a lesson you taught me all those years ago. A lesson that has allowed me to pursue my dream career, raise three kids, and surmount all manner of obstacles—from divorce and single motherhood to earthquakes, blizzards, and dotcoms.

Simply put: You taught me how to think. As a sixteen-year-old obsessed with clothes, parties, and boys (not necessarily in that order) thinking was not foremost on my mind during my junior year of high school. Much less thinking deeply about such esoterica as Emersonian self-reliance, Shakespearean simile, and Aristotelian unity.

I believed these subjects to be completely irrelevant at the time, preoccupied as I was by more pressing girlish concerns such as landing attractive dates for every (equally important) Saturday night and talking my parents out of my midnight curfew. Still, despite this seeming irrelevance, you drew me in, challenging me to master the mysteries of logic, independent thought, and critical thinking. You taught me to honor the poets and philosophers among us, past and present—and to honor the poet and philosopher in myself. Most important, you taught me to believe in the sound of my own voice and the soundness of my own arguments.

Ask any of the girls in our class and they'd tell you that I was teacher's pet—but they'd also tell you that I'd earned it. It was neither an enviable nor envied role; you were too demanding, too intellectual, too uncompromising. You scared them. You never scared me. I admired you, respected you, emulated you—but I never feared you. As a military brat reared by a colonel, I was used to the demanding and the uncompromising. And I craved intellectual stimulation. For me, you were tough but endlessly fascinating; I loved the way your mind worked. I wanted to learn to think the way you thought—and you were happy to teach me.

After graduation I left New Orleans, and have been back only rarely since. Yet I treasure my ties to the 278-year-old girls' school where you taught, always reading the alumnae newsletters and attending class reunions with an affection that borders on excessive sentimentality. I particularly appreciate any news of you. I was not surprised to hear that you went on to serve as principal of the academy, and later as Mother Superior of the convent. You were born to lead grownups—not sixteen-year-old girls.

As a grown-up myself now, I am grateful that your fine intellect, sharp determination, and dogged pursuit of excellence were once wasted on my sixteen-year-old self. You taught me how to think—and that's what school is supposed to be all about.

Long after I've forgotten almost everything else I learned in high school, I remember that "a foolish consistency is the hobgoblin of little minds" and that "the course of true love never did run smooth" and that "action is eloquence" and that "hope is a waking dream." I owe whatever success I've enjoyed to your insistence that I learn the triple-whammy arts of Emersonian self-reliance, Shakespearean simile, and Aristotelian unity.

If only you'd known as much about husbands.

BEST,

Paula Munier
Pembroke, Massachusetts

A writer, editor, and novelist, Paula Munier is mother to Alexis, Gregory, and Mikey. She lives in rural Massachusetts in a lakeside cottage with her family, two dogs, and a cat.

The Prize Teacher

🍎 By Jenny Block 🍎

Dear Mrs. Christopher,

You always had prizes. You were the first teacher I ever had who really got it. Kids don't like school. Kids don't care about the big picture. Kids aren't interested in learning for learning's sake. Kids like prizes. And you had them, secreted away in a gigantic see-through bag high atop the supply closet in our classroom.

I loved to stare at that bag and try to discern what secret treasures lay within. The whole third-grade class at Bakersfield Elementary in Aberdeen, Maryland, wanted those prizes, and you knew it. And that is what made you a genius.

I can still picture you, smiling and enthusiastic. "You may work on the activity folders after you have finished your in-class assignments neatly and correctly. Finish a set of activities, and you get to pick a prize," you told us.

My dad called you a firecracker. Your sparks were contagious, and your peppy instructions were all I needed to hear. My handwriting had never been better. My speed had never been faster. And my knowledge of classroom material had never been sharper. You were a whiz. You tapped the one part of a child that no other teacher dared tap—the desire to win stuff.

Your methods were a double whammy in terms of teaching and learning opportunities. The activity folders were filled with what really amounted to additional in-class assignments. They were usually a little more fun, like crossword puzzles or word finds, but they always related to the class material. And even when they didn't resemble games, we didn't care. We were happy sitting at the activity table and working toward the chance to dig our hands into the sacred prize bag. Nothing could have put a damper on our determination.

The funny thing was that the prizes were the oddest assortment of items: miniature picture frames, bags of colorful potpourri, key chains, and purse-size mirrors. They were freebies you'd gotten in the mail, junk from the bargain bin at Ames, and giveaways you picked up at conferences! I was unaware of the origins of the prizes until much later, when I was, strangely enough, substitute teaching for your class fifteen years after I had been in it. You still had that giant prize bag, and it still seemed to work.

I don't ever recall your having to lecture the class about not doing our homework or not doing well on a test. Your prize concept worked for 90 percent of your students. Of course, that wasn't enough for you—you wanted that other 10 percent. We would sometimes see you out in the hall, through the small, square window in our classroom door, speaking to a student who was not doing well and never worked on the activity folders.

"Excuse me just a moment, class," you would say as you stepped into the hall, closing the door behind you. We couldn't hear you, but we imagined the conversation for ourselves. "Now Travis, I just don't understand. Why aren't you doing your work? Don't you want to win prizes like the other students?"

We couldn't understand either. Most of us would have done anything to get at that giant bag. My best friend and I certainly would have, working as we did like maniacs to earn as many prizes as possible. "I used to scramble to make up more activity folders because you and Mary Beth went through them like crazy," you told me years later. I might have apologized for creating more work if you had been anyone else, but I knew that you had taken our enthusiasm as the highest compliment.

Naturally, you wanted us to have a desire to learn for the sheer joy of learning. But you were a realist. You knew that if you could motivate us externally, we would become motivated internally, making knowledge the sole prize. You couldn't have been more right. I continue to be an excellent student. And now, I'm a pretty good teacher myself, teaching college students who would rather have their teeth pulled without Novocain than take a writing class. I don't have a prize bag. But I do use your methodology.

I don't know if you teach anymore, Mrs. Christopher, but I do know that you were one heck of a teacher. Intelligent, witty, generous, and creative. You never cared about how unorthodox your teaching methods might be or how colleagues might react to them. Your sole desire was for us to learn, and we did. More than you'll ever know.

WITH WARMEST REGARDS,

Jenny Block
Dallas, Texas

Jenny Block is a writer living in Dallas, Texas. Her work has recently appeared in Virginia Living *magazine,* Richmond *magazine,* Style Weekly *magazine, and on* www.literarymama.com. *She also appears in* It's a Girl: Women Writers on Raising Daughters.

Keeping It Light

By Renee Evans

Dear Mrs. Frei,

Returning to school had never been part of my plan. Certainly not at the "old age" of forty-eight. I had expected my life to wrap around being a housewife and mother until the kids were grown. Then the idea was to sit in a rocking chair on the front porch as I grew older, and eventually retire in my comfortable nest. But before I could get ensconced in a cane-back rocker, the nest fell apart and I had to do something I'd never counted on—figure out how to get a job. With no work experience or college degree, and facing a divorce, I was feeling very old and entirely overwhelmed.

Although massage school was not the daunting experience that college would have been, it seemed huge at that point in my life. For me, and most of the other women in my Gainesville, Georgia class, the mere idea of removing our clothes to practice massage on each other was intimidating. What was I thinking?

From the very first day of school, you walked into our classroom with a big smile and a sense of humor that would get us—and especially me—through the uncertainties we faced.

The school was located in the historic part of our small town. It was an old southern-style two-story house with a wraparound veranda. During orientation, you told us the house was haunted. "Now don't be surprised if you see a young girl appear and disappear," you laughed. "Especially on the staircase. She's harmless. Actually not everyone gets to see her, so if you do, you're one of the lucky ones."

Nothing like feeling lucky in a haunted massage school.

I'll never forget the day we started abdominal massage. The first thing that morning, you came into class and stood in front of your desk with a perfectly straight face. Suddenly, we heard a loud fart. All eyes were on you. And then we heard it again. Nobody made a sound. You just stood there for a few seconds and let us wonder what to do, and then you laughed and set a fart cup down on your desk.

Next you whipped out a whoopee cushion, gave it a squeeze, and tossed it onto one of the massage tables. Then you dug into your bag and pulled out a children's book about animal farts and passed it around the room. We got the message: it was okay, and even expected, that some of us were going to fart when we started massaging abdomens.

When it was time for career day, you told us to prepare for a job interview. Half of us were to play the role of employer and the other half were applicants. We had instructions to dress professionally and be prepared to answer questions as if it were a real job interview. We were dreading it, but then we got together and came up with a plan to do something different. When career day came around, we dressed up all right . . .

We showed up to class dressed as a hooker, a slob with blacked-out teeth, a dumb blonde, an airy-fairy (that was me), and one of the women, who had a degree in theater, gave a hilarious rendition of an interview with a redneck.

All day long, we gave all the wrong answers, and career day was a big joke. You sat at the back of the room and laughed at everything we did. Not only did you let us turn your serious class into a farce, you gave us a good grade for it. No matter what came up, we could always count on you to show us how to keep it light, and now we were showing you what we'd learned.

I'll never forget how you got us through our anxieties so easily. You helped me as I moved on in life and faced many changes. It's been many years since massage school, and I'm no longer a therapist, but I will always remember the wonderful massage techniques you taught me, and appreciate the way you taught all of us to find humor and to keep it light.

I can't say I've done it flawlessly, or even easily, but your example has made a huge difference in the way I look at life. So thank you, Mrs. Frei, for being there as a wonderful teacher and an inspiring person, in more ways than you'll ever know.

BEST,

Renee Evans
Portland, Oregon

Based in Portland, Oregon, Renee Evans is an intuitive guide and works with BETAR vibrational music therapy.

The Story of Mrs. Bishop
🍎 BY MONICA KROPF 🍎

The first time I walked in our class she was nice to us. She has been nice the whole year. She never was mean to the class.

She is the best teacher that I have had. The class always had fun with her. She does a lot of fun things like the art she has the class do. I like evry thing about her. She likes my cursive not my hand writting. But she likes evry body and she has good adatood.

She mackes life easy to do math. She will help you solve problems. She has a nice friend mrs miller. If you are in 2nd grade and are goining to 3rd grade you get arcadia dollers 100, 50,10, 5 and 1 doller bills. You also get a wonderful teacher mrs Miller or mrs Bishop. You get to do fun activates. this year we got devided in to teams and played serviver it was hard but my team won.

You get to wach movies almost evry day a lot of old fashen movies there are four groups frog, butterfly, ladybug and draginfly. I always had fun and that is my favrite teacher Mrs Bishop.

THANK YOU FOR BEING MY TEACHER!

MONica KRopf

Toledo, Oregon

Monica Kropf is a nine-year-old who likes to swim and play video games.

Beyond the Wall

By Birgit Nielsen

Dear Mr. Dworaczek,

In 1969, I was in your fourth-grade geography class
at Anne-Frank-Grundschule in what was then West
Berlin, Germany. You walked into class with a stack
of books and an atlas under your arm, and spoke about
the ages of mountains, deltas, streams, and sediment as
if these things were of vital importance.

And they are.

How does one explain human migration and
settlement in areas of the planet that are naturally flat
and arid? It seems to me now a rather tall question for
fourth graders. But you explained to us the concept of
irrigation and the invention of the bucket-wheel, and
more importantly, that the rise of powerful nations
historically depended on their ability to feed their
people. With conviction, your hands swept across
maps and illustrations of erosion, soil composition,
and tectonic plates. You pounded the blackboard
and strode up and down between our desks in deep
contemplation.

On your rounds through the classroom, you
walked between the desks with your hands in your
pockets, your sleeves rolled up, exposing your dry, scaly
elbows. When you passed the wall-mounted maps, you
reached up and unfurled the dusty crinkled paper to
test our knowledge of the geographical makeup of the

country. You pointed at green, tan, and brown areas and said, "Do you know what this is? This is your country. How can there be peace if this abomination of the Wall is standing? There is only one country—one united country. What we have now, two separate nations, is a travesty. We must never accept it. To accept it is to accept persecution and torture."

My family had moved to West Berlin only the year before. In the provincial town we left for Berlin, the reaction of many was hushed or a little shocked that we should be so daring. My teacher there broke into tears over the news, thinking my parents were about to deliver me into the hands of Communists, and that we would summarily be shot on the first weekend.

When I asked my parents what was so peculiar about Berlin, they repeatedly assured me that "everything will be fine," and "It's perfectly safe, you know. Don't worry." In daily life, this was certainly true. It was evidently untrue in every aspect, because there you were in my geography class, abandoning the lesson plan, thundering to a room full of nine- and ten-year-olds about injustice, cruel division, and opposition.

It occurred to me many years later that there was nothing coincidental about your going off on a tangent. You rightly looked at us as the first generation with no living memory of an undivided Berlin, and it was indeed vital to you that we should be taught not to accept given circumstances, lest we grew up gullible and complacent. More importantly, you were not so arrogant to think a roomful of children would not understand what you were talking about.

You were not a young man then, and would be quite old now if you are still among us. I do hope you were alive on November 9, 1989, when the Wall came down. I thought of you then.

Thank you, Mr. Dworaczek, for teaching me that serious inquiry into the world we live in sparks enthusiasm, and that idealism is not a frivolous concept.

SINCERELY,

Birgit Nielsen
Portland, Oregon

Birgit Nielsen (MFA, Goddard) works as a translator and writer. Recent publications include Steeped in the World of Tea *(Interlink, 2004). She is donating her share of the proceeds from this book to* http://www.futuresforchildren.org/.

Carpe Diem

🍎 By Danielle Mutarelli 🍎

Dear Mrs. Rodriguez,

I was a chatterbox in second grade, just as I am now.
But ironically, it was in your class at South Yarmouth
Elementary School on Cape Cod that I learned to
listen, and that's when the true learning began. It was
1979, and it seemed as if we had spent the previous
two years as students acquiring tools, and now you
were showing us what we could do with them. The
world suddenly appeared before my eyes.

You were fresh and fearless as a young teacher,
and remarkably adventurous as you sought to find
your stride and your own personal style. New teaching
methods and materials were brought forth to us with
an unsurpassed energy and exuberance.

In the mornings, before the first bell, you would
let us play records and dance. We'd cluster in the back
of the class around the record player that you'd brought
from home. Underneath a clothesline of drying
artwork, we moved in blissful, rhythmless wonder. I've
danced with such abandonment only a handful of times
since then. You knew how positively we would react,
and so for those precious mornings, you let us dance.

Do you remember the routine the other girls
and I made up to go along with Barry Manilow's
"Copacabana"? It was so campy, and you loved it. Your

brown hair would swing and catch the light as you tossed it back, laughing.

We lost one of our own the following year. I'm sure you remember Chris Kaldis, taken too soon by cancer in the third grade. It was because of this loss that you began to take a class photo each year that you'd save in your filing cabinet—each face a gem. You told me this the day I came to visit you, when I myself was considering becoming a teacher. You said we were the class that changed you—the class that enabled you to finally focus on each face that passed before you. Your students were no longer a blur to you, lumped together under one approach, but individuals with unique strengths and weaknesses. We came to you like waves to the shore.

We had a moment together that day, talking about my future while thinking back to our shared past. You pointed to a desk and said, "I believe that's where you sat."

It was such a special moment, brief and fleeting. But we saw it as such and caught it, holding on tight to that single moment. You taught me how to do that.

SINCERELY YOURS,

Danielle Giardino Mutarelli
Merrimack, New Hampshire

Danielle Mutarelli is an aspiring young writer who divides her writing time between fiction and nonfiction, loving both equally. She presently lives in New Hampshire with her husband and their three-year-old son.

The Opera and I

By Laurene Liljenquist Arnett

Dear Dr. Christensen,

It's been almost sixty-one years since I enrolled in your Opera Appreciation class just for fun. The only thing I knew about opera was that the tenors sounded good, but the sopranos screeched. I wanted to know more.

You taught the class in the library at Utah State Agricultural College, when enrollment was not only low, but 80 percent women. There were probably about a dozen in the class, and we listened to operas on long-playing (LP) records, following printed scores with English translations below the original words. Our textbook was *The Victor Book of the Opera*.

You took me into another world as I drank in the beauty of the music, the drama of the action, and learned to recognize arias and hum along with them. I had no part-time job that quarter, so whenever nothing else was pressing, I went to the library and listened all by myself. At times there would be another class in the large room, but it was always far enough away from the record player that I could don earphones and listen without disrupting anyone.

USAC's school year was divided into quarters then, so we couldn't study many operas. We did study *Aida*, *La Traviata*, *Il Trovatore*, *Rigoletto*, *Faust*, *Carmen*, *La Boheme*, *Cavalleria Rusticana*, *Pagliacci,* and touched on *The Barber of Seville*. I found myself loving them all, because you made them come alive for me as we listened and discussed the characters, the plot, the music, and the composers. You helped me to recognize the arias from each opera, to know which character was singing, the composer's name, and the opera title. "This," you said, "is what you will be tested on."

When finals neared, several of us students met in the library to "cram." One of the LPs we tried sounded funny.

"Oh, there's a crack in the record," somebody said.

"I think I can recognize that aria," I responded, much to my amazement. "You know an aria by its melody."

One of the girls replied, "But they all sound alike!"

You can lead a horse to water, I thought, *but drinking is a matter of choice.* Dr. Christensen led us well. The rest was up to us.

The test was just what you told us to expect. We could not see where you placed the phonograph needle, nor which record you played, but we listened to the beauty of those marvelous records (which would sound pretty tinny today), decided what was playing, and wrote our answers accordingly.

When I handed in my test paper, you asked me if I could stay a moment after class. After all students turned in their papers and left, you turned to me.

"I have an important appointment right away, and the grades must be posted this evening," you said. "Can you grade these test papers for me?"

I said I could, and you turned to leave.

"But don't I need the test key?" I asked.

It was then that you paid me one of the highest compliments I've ever received. "Use your own paper," you said. You paused, pulled a test key from your briefcase, and quickly checked my answers. You knew me better than I had thought. I actually *could* have used my own.

I married the next June and eventually became mother to seven wonderful children, who often heard operatic music from my own few LPs. When our youngest child started first grade, I re-enrolled in college (along with my oldest son), and became an English teacher.

No, I did not teach opera. I never sang in an opera. As yet, I have never even attended a grand opera, though I've watched a few on television. But the love for the operas you guided me through proved to be one of the truly enriching experiences in my life.

I'VE BEEN FOREVER GRATEFUL TO YOU,
DR. CHRISTENSEN,
AND IT'S HIGH TIME I TOLD YOU.

Laurene Liljenquist Arnett
Gilbert, Arizona

An octogenarian, mother of seven, grandmother of twenty-eight, and great grandmother of twenty-two, Laurene Liljenquist Arnett loves life, learning, teaching, reading, writing, needlework, church and community service. She willingly accepts almost any good challenge, and still dreams of getting a Ph.D.

A Room with a View

🍎 By Jenny Lentz 🍎

Dear Mrs. Ottewell,

You were my teacher from third through fifth grades, at the Montessori School in Greenville, South Carolina. You terrified and intimidated us. Every time we opened our mouths, we feared your response, but at the same time, you awed us.

At age eight, I requested permission to go home with a stomachache, stating, "I don't feel good." You refused to grant permission until I realized what was incorrect about my sentence. Finally, with the corrected, "I don't feel well," you granted permission and nurturing sympathy. It was common for you to stop us in midsentence, especially if we ever said "like" (as in, "I have a question about, like, what it is we're supposed to do"). You never hesitated to interject a correction whenever we spoke.

Along with grammar lessons, however, you provided us with a global awareness and understanding that we had not encountered elsewhere in our small corner of South Carolina. You were exotic—a New Zealander who was the wife of a famous astronomer. And your worldliness showed, as the drawers of your classroom overflowed with stamped envelopes from your global correspondence.

For our monthly geography reports, you permitted each student to select relevant stamps and soak them in special bowls to loosen them from the envelopes. I still have my stamps, from Kenya, Bolivia, Costa Rica, France, West Germany, Brazil, Australia, Sweden, Madagascar, and others. What amazed me most was that you weren't a stamp collector purchasing unused stamps. Your stamps were from letters and postcards you'd received from friends all over the world.

You enthralled us with tales of your archaeological digs, research expeditions, and mountain-climbing adventures, showing us your collections of ancient pottery shards, fossilized dinosaur remains, ashes from Mt. St. Helens, and souvenirs from your journeys to every continent. You taught us to respect and admire other cultures, and to assist others in need.

Do you remember Reimer Priester, the hyperactive kid who was always getting into trouble? He currently serves in the Peace Corps in Guinea, living in less-than-ideal conditions and promoting AIDS awareness in order to improve the world. He never forgot the lessons you taught him.

I also have you to thank for what I have become. In third grade, you noticed my spelling proficiency, so you allowed me to be in the fourth-grade spelling class; in fourth grade, I was in the fifth-grade spelling class. In fifth grade, there was no sixth-grade spelling class, so instead of spelling, you had me write short stories. You were the first person to foster and assist me with my writing. You read and edited every story, your encouragement unwavering.

You opened up so many worlds to us. You took us through the woods and pointed out the names of every flower and tree. You taught us Latin and history, literature and vocabulary, astronomy and science, art and poetry. You seemed to know everything. I have never encountered anyone who knew so much about so many things, and who presented it with such wonder and fascination. You made us realize the value of knowledge, learning, and the world.

You could probably have done anything with your life, with your knowledge and intelligence— something earning a far greater income than from teaching at that small South Carolina school. But it was always clear how much you loved to teach, to inspire us toward greatness. I am eternally grateful that you became a teacher and showed me the wonders of the world.

It is through words, through writing, that I try to make a difference, to change opinions, increase awareness, inspire, and promote understanding of other cultures, societies, and people. Reimer and I, in different ways, are using your teachings and urgings to improve the world you so adore.

You had said that when you retired, you would grow a magnificent garden. I hope that is where you are now, with your wide-brimmed straw hat and wispy white hair, and the smile that I always relished because it meant I'd made you proud. I hope that as you admire your snapdragons, dahlias, chrysanthemums, and orchids, you realize how much you changed the lives of your students, and that you never regret your decision to become a teacher.

You did change the world, Mrs. Ottewell, through your students, and we're continuing your mission to make the world a better place.

WITH GRATITUDE,

Jenny Lentz
Philadelphia, Pennsylvania

Jenny Lentz holds a B.A. in English and Creative Writing from Bryn Mawr College and is a graduate of the South Carolina Governor's School for the Arts Creative Writing program. She currently works in human resources in Philadelphia. Her fiction has appeared in several print and online literary magazines.

A Life Saved and a Life Lived

🍎 By Jeff Shantz 🍎

Dear Mr. Kriz,

I hope this letter finds you well, wherever you happen to be in this great world. If you are still the man I knew all those years ago, my guess would be that I might find you somewhere on the Left Bank of that romantic capital, Paris, arguing with the ghosts of Jean-Paul Sartre and Albert Camus. It was twenty years ago that you introduced this introverted young misfit to the great existential philosophers, and in doing so, changed my life.

I could never have expected when I first entered your class that you would open up thrilling new worlds of imagination and ideas, while helping me get a handle on the day-to-day reality I was living. You had a reputation as an eccentric, and many students avoided your class because you were supposedly "too tough."

You could not have imagined the state I was in when this shy and awkward kid took a seat in your class (off to the side, in a nice inconspicuous spot). My parents had split up only the month before your class started, and I was something of a mess. All of the certainties of my life, the foundations on which I had grown, had fallen apart piece by piece. I no longer trusted anything or, more to the point, anyone. Like a character in one of the absurdist plays you encouraged your students to read, I felt like I was gradually losing touch with my past, catching glimpses of it only through the words of others as I sat in Hell's waiting room (to borrow from my favorite Sartre play).

It's always easy for teenagers to feel sorry for themselves—it's something they excel at. Unfortunately, this impulse often has dire consequences unless someone comes along and offers direction, or perhaps more importantly, recognizes that with growth and change comes a certain degree of alienation. That was what you provided—and not in the patronizing way that guidance counselors tended to offer. You were never dismissive, realizing that even our weaknesses and failings could become strengths if they encouraged us to learn, develop, and take the pursuit of ideas and understanding in new and untried directions.

You taught me that alienation had its place, and that absurdity was part of the human condition. More importantly, you helped me to recognize that uncertainty has its merits. The unknown is not something to be feared or shunned, but something to reach out to—to explore. This insight, and the courage that develops with it, is something I've carried with me throughout my life. I entered your class confused and afraid and left it with a craving to embrace the world.

As a blue-collar kid, I was used to being treated with low expectations from other teachers, who always let it be known—often subtly, sometimes more explicitly—that my friends and I could settle for less, or be happy with something much less than the best. But you pushed us to do more, to raise our expectations and challenge ourselves intellectually. The fact that you did this in another language, encouraging us to read complex French authors in the original form, only added to the excitement of discovery. That's something that I've taken far beyond your classroom, carrying it with me throughout my life.

During my years in graduate school—the first in my family to ever attend—I often reflected on how I ended up there and why I'd taken that route. And the beginning of an answer always came back to you and your little class with the "tough" philosophers.

So thank you, Mr. Kriz. You looked beyond the cloudy demeanor, saw a spark, and took the time to fuel it. With verve, and yes, a certain eccentricity, you reached my creative core and started a fire that's been burning ever since.

In writing this, I have to say I felt a twinge of regret for not having done it sooner, but at the same time, I knew that for you, it would be all right. You would understand, as you always did. For any bird to truly fly, it has to leave the nest.

Here's to you, Mr. Kriz. I raise a toast of the Left Bank's finest in your honor. And while you're at it, say "Hi" to Sartre for me.

WITH APPRECIATION FOR A LIFE SAVED AND A LIFE LIVED,

Jeff Shantz
Toronto, Ontario, Canada

Jeff Shantz currently lives in Toronto with his partner and their daughter and son. He teaches at York University and also hosts a weekly radio program on community station CHRY in Toronto.

The Psychology of Ethics

By Wendy S. Komancheck

Dear Dr. Burkhart,

You retired last June, and in the Eastern Lancaster County School District's newsletter, it was written that you've touched numerous students during your years as a classroom teacher and administrator. I am one of those inspired students—a quiet, insecure girl who found her voice in your classroom.

I took your psychology class in my sophomore year at Garden Spot High School in New Holland, Pennsylvania. It was 1985, and I was intimidated by you because you were the only teacher who had a Ph.D. I was afraid that your class would be too academically challenging, and you would tell me that everything I believed in was false. I was certain that you would say I was dumb, naive, or a flunky.

But I was dead wrong.

On the first day of class, you greeted us warmly and encouraged us to express our opinions. You listened to us and challenged us, but not in a bad way. Instead, you made us think about different psychological concepts and case studies. I remember sitting in class talking about a woman who was slowly murdered in New York City. The account in our textbook related how this woman was repeatedly stabbed during the day. She tried to get help from her neighbors but was turned away by everyone. Eventually, her attacker returned to kill her.

I read ahead in the textbook that day, and remember thinking, "This is interesting. I can't believe that nobody helped her. Surely, anyone would help a poor woman being stabbed in the middle of the day. You only needed to be afraid at night."

To my surprise, a few days later, you used that incident as a platform for a situational ethics discussion. It scared me. I didn't want to believe that I couldn't trust my own neighbors to protect me from an out-of-control world because they were affected by "group ethics."

"Why do you think that nobody would help this woman who was being pursued by a man who eventually stabbed her to death in the middle of the street in broad daylight?" you asked.

The question spurred my imagination. I began to consider what it must have felt like running door to door, banging and pleading for help. Why did the men refuse to open their doors to rescue this woman? Couldn't the women empathize with that helpless victim? What was the victim feeling? Was she terrified, feeling the pain of her cuts as she tried to run while she was bleeding? What was she feeling as she lay dying on the street with no one to comfort her or rescue her, while people numbly watched behind their curtains?

You refused to answer those questions. You wanted us to think about group ethics and what motivates people to stand behind locked doors while a young woman bleeds to death at the hands of her murderer.

"I'm not telling you what to think. I want you to decide what they should have done. Why do you think her neighbors ignored her pleas for help?"

Immediately I raised my hand and said, "I would help her. I would let her in my house."

Instead of putting me down, you asked me another question: "Wouldn't you be afraid of the intruder barging his way into your home and killing you both? Or coming to get you later for helping her?" I thought about that, and yes, to my shame, I would have been afraid of retaliation by this mad stranger.

That lesson of why people don't get involved, because they fear retaliation, has stuck with me throughout my life. Class ended that day without anyone reaching a conclusion as to why the people in that New York neighborhood didn't come to the aid of a helpless woman. But I became more confident that day in your classroom, and I took more of your classes in the following years.

You inspired me to be confident in my opinions, and I became a teacher because of the inspiration that you provided for me. I can only hope that I can be the inspiration for my students that you were to me.

BEST WISHES IN YOUR RETIREMENT,

Wendy Komancheck
Ephrata, Pennsylvania

Wendy S. Komancheck is a professional tutor and writer. She lives in Pennsylvania with her family.

Spark of Inspiration

🍎 By Rick Sutherland 🍎

Dear Mrs. Howarth,

I was a student in your English class my junior year of high school in 1968. Reasonably bright but profoundly unmotivated, I floundered from class to class, searching for a few elusive sparks. I found one of them in your class.

I wasn't inspired by reading classic literature, nor was I overly enthusiastic about the esoteric subtleties of sentence conjugation (although I can still fake it). The spark I found was that I could make you laugh.

While I could hardly be described as a class clown, I tended to pepper written assignments with humorous observations that had absolutely nothing to do with the content. I completely ignored your messages in the margins of returned papers that read, *"When you get to college, instructors will expect a serious approach to your work,"* and *"College instructors have no sense of humor."* In a few years, I would find that your warnings would prove to be 100 percent correct, but I was young and irrepressible, and I'm sure you knew it—and so permitted it.

Toward the end of the school year, you began a class with comments addressing where each of us thought we were headed in life. With that in mind, you asked us to spend the rest of the class period writing about what was going on in our lives right now. Pens popped, pencils were sharpened, and fresh theme paper appeared like snowfall.

Hmmm. What's going on in my life right now? Well, right now I'm surrounded by a bunch of students writing about what's going on in their lives. Right now, Gary Peterson is waving his hand like a second grader, asking if we can write about our families, and I'm thinking, well isn't your family in your life right now, and you're saying, yes, you can write about your family, and I'm thinking, as opposed to someone else's family? Donna Lawrence, sitting in the aisle next to me, keeps crossing and re-crossing her legs and chewing on the end of her pencil because apparently, she can't think of anything going on her life right now. I'm also noticing that right now, Donna Lawrence has great legs.

I kept this up for half an hour, and finally finished up with:

Right now, just about nothing is going on in my life, except that I've written six pages about what is going on in my life, and my pen is running low on ink. So, I'm going to stop and turn this paper in. Then I'm going to try to try to take a nap for the last ten minutes of this class without getting caught, which won't be easy, considering that I just told you I was going to do it.

The next day, I walked into class with a certain amount of trepidation. Had I gone too far? As soon as we were seated, you stood up with a slip of paper in your hand and called my name. I walked up to the front of the class and you handed me the slip—a library pass.

"Rick, I want you to go to the library for fifteen minutes," you said.

This isn't good, I thought.

"But . . . but . . . ," I stammered.

"Go."

I went, and I worried for fifteen minutes. I think I probably stretched it out to twenty. When I returned, the entire class turned toward me and collectively cracked up.

Oh God, she read it to them.

Smiling at me, you said, "If you don't mind, I'd like to keep the paper you wrote yesterday for teaching my classes next year." I was astonished, vaguely embarrassed, and absurdly proud.

During the thirty years that have followed, I've pursued my passion for writing, and my desire to provoke the unforgettable responses I got from you. And if by some chance you read this, I hope I made you laugh again.

WISHING YOU THE BEST,

Rick Sutherland

The Oregon Coast

Rick Sutherland left a career in print management and sales to focus on writing, production, and editing. He has coauthored several books and makes his home in the Pacific Northwest with his better half, Barb, a goofy greyhound, and a quartet of felines.

The Extent of Your Harvest

🍎 By Nan Schindler Russell 🍎

Dear Mr. Jones,

You were my writing topic recently. You see, I'm now a self-syndicated columnist, writing a life reflections column called *In the Scheme of Things*. Back in eighth grade, you gave me much to reflect on, and forty-some years later, you still do. Writing this column was my way of saying thank you for impacting my life. My column began like this:

"You intimidated me. Your deep voice and quick-firing speech left me uncertain and wondering if I'd understood your directions. It was clear you weren't going to repeat them. It was also clear you expected your new eighth-grade class to quickly engage in your topic of choice—social studies."

By the end of that hour, you were expounding on your standards and expectations for the year, and I understood it was not going to be the kind of class I was used to. For a shy thirteen-year-old, it was overwhelming.

Yet, I worked harder for you that year than I'd ever worked for any teacher. There was something about you that brought out the best in me, and by the end of the year, my feelings of intimidation had quietly morphed into feelings of inspiration. I learned to love your class, not because I loved the subject, but because I loved how you made me feel—smart, curious, confident, and eager to learn.

Despite that, when you kept me after class the last week of school, I was nervous, and then stunned, when you asked me to be editor for the next school yearbook. "You can write and organize and lead," you said matter-of-factly. "You're a natural for the job."

No one had ever told me that I could do those things. On that hot June day, you changed my life with your encouraging words. You saw in me what I never saw in myself. You were faculty advisor for the yearbook, and the next year, as I served as editor, you pulled from me the abilities you knew I had.

During that year, I learned more than how to edit the yearbook. I learned how encouraging words could change my self-view. You planted the seeds of possibility in my head. With a few words, you changed what I thought I could do or even be. I don't know if you are the person who helped me become a writer, but I do know your encouraging words allowed me to harbor the thought that I could. And now, I am.

When someone believes in you, it changes you. They see in you what you don't see in yourself. They hold a mirror up to offer a glimpse of your reflection. Encouraging words open possibilities, increase determination, and awaken dreams. Mr. Jones, you and dozens of bosses, coaches, family, friends, and strangers have done that for me, all of their words impacting my life far beyond their encounter.

In the scheme of things, encouraging words don't have an expiration date. I don't remember much about eighth-grade social studies, but I do recall a few words that nurtured my self-esteem and unveiled my talents.

There are people who stomp out seeds of possibility, and there are people who plant them. But being a planter and offering a few encouraging words of your own has one residual aftereffect: you may never know the extent of your harvest.

IN YOUR DEBT,

Nan Russell
Whitefish, Montana

Nan Schindler Russell is living her dream in Montana after twenty years in management on the East Coast. Currently writing her first book, Winning at Working: 10 Lessons Shared, *Nan is a writer, columnist, and speaker.* www.nanrussell.com

The Mastery of Grace

🍎 By Dianna Graveman 🍎

Dear Sister Marheineke,

When I was in college working on my teaching degree, several of my instructors asked me to write about one of my own teachers who had made a difference—somebody who had influenced me to become a teacher myself. I always had a hard time with that, because I didn't really enjoy school when I was young. The only teachers I remembered were the ones I didn't particularly like. *Who are these teachers,* I thought, *who have such profound impact on their students?*

And then I thought of you.

You were a dear friend to my husband and his family, and you had stood by my side when I was confirmed in the Catholic Church many years ago. You had also attended my wedding and the baptism of my children.

I had spent years watching little ones flock to your side, in awe of the love and joy that seemed to surround you and envelop all others who spent time in your company. Often I encountered your former students, both young and older, who told me of the positive effect you had on their lives.

After receiving my teaching degree, I was thrilled to be offered a job at Academy of the Sacred Heart in St. Charles, Missouri, the very school where you taught. I couldn't imagine working with a more accomplished teacher or supportive mentor, and I looked forward to learning from the best.

As the beginning of the school year approached and I nervously prepared lessons for my very first students, you often visited my classroom, complimenting me on my fresh ideas and offering encouragement for the year ahead—high praise, coming from such a revered and respected educator. I never told you how much that meant to me.

Finally, the first day of school arrived, and I was jittery with excitement. Everyone was to gather in the gym for an assembly and opening address by our headmistress. As I led my class of third graders into the room and seated them neatly in rows on the floor, I thought I had prepared well. I'd studied the curriculum and textbooks, and I knew the material I was supposed to teach. I had designed creative and interesting lessons and activities, and my behavior plan was in place.

Suddenly I realized that everybody—faculty and students—were bowing their heads and had begun to recite loudly and clearly a prayer I had never learned. My eight-year-old charges looked up at me, their teacher, for guidance—and I had no idea what I was supposed to be saying! I lowered my head and moved my lips silently, hoping nobody would notice my ineptitude.

But you noticed. On my desk the following morning was a small card printed with a prayer for the intercession of St. Philippine Duchesne, and on the back was a little yellow Post-it note on which you had written:

> *Dear Dianna,*
> *This is the prayer we recited yesterday at assembly.*
> *Love,*
> *Anna Mae*

I should have been embarrassed at having been found out, but instead, I felt blessed. You were watching out for me, and I knew you would help me find my way in this business of educating children. I was never graced with the opportunity to sit at a desk in your classroom and learn under your dedicated and compassionate direction like so many others over the years. Nevertheless, I was your student, and you were my teacher. And there was still so much to learn.

Love and gratitude always,

Dianna Graveman
St. Charles, Missouri

Dianna Graveman is a third-grade teacher and holds a master of fine arts degree in writing. She lives in Missouri with her husband and three almost-grown children.

From Whack to Sharpest Tack

By Linda Bruno

Dear Mrs. Scarbery,

Whack! The ruler hit my knuckles with what was probably only a light tap, but it felt like a baseball bat. It's my first memory of life in your first-grade class as you expressed your disappointment that the letter X I was trying so hard to print had turned out crooked. As I look back, you were probably just trying to get my attention—and get my attention you did!

Nowadays, of course, you would likely be criticized for such a "harsh" punishment, but I never questioned your authority to do whatever you felt necessary to help me learn. If the same scene played out today, my feelings would be no different. I knew you took your job of teaching young minds seriously.

Kindergarten was virtually unheard of in those days, and certainly not required. It was 1961 at Jackson Center Local Schools, in Jackson Center, Ohio. My only preparation before entering your class had been at home, where my mother was busy taking care of a house, two older children, two huge gardens, and all the extra work that comes with living in the country. There simply wasn't time to spend on lessons at home, so over the next several weeks, I practiced writing my letters on my own so their crookedness would no longer disappoint you.

And then one day, I heard you say, "Why can't you be more like Cheryl Pellman?" It was a comment that was invariably followed by, "She's sharp as a tack."

I had tasted "comparison" for the first time, and it was a bitter pill to swallow. But, as most medicine does, it ended up benefiting me tremendously. You had thrown out the gauntlet, so to speak, and I eagerly accepted the challenge. I worked hard to prove that I *could* be like Cheryl Pellman. I studied as much as a first grader can, and did my very best work for you.

As others were disciplined with forays into the cloakroom, I remained sitting quietly, whether from fear of you or my parents, I'm not sure which. I had been taught to respect my elders, and to be honest, you seemed ancient to me! I only knew, as a six-year-old knows, that what I was doing seemed to please you. And while you never really acknowledged that you were pleased, your lack of displeasure was enough incentive for me to keep doing what I was doing.

What began as a less-than-auspicious start to my education developed into a love of the proverbial "readin', writin', and 'rithmetic." Soon enough, first grade was finished and I had come through it unscathed, but for that initial incident with the ruler. What had changed, though, was what held my interest.

Now that the longed-for summer recess had arrived, I found myself bored with my previous summertime activities. At age six, I could often be found standing by the mailbox at the end of our country lane, waiting anxiously for the mailman and his precious cargo: *The Weekly Reader,* a periodical that contained infinite treasure for this young mind. Simply printed in black and white, it held more allure for me than any video game ever could, even if they had been invented at that time.

Over the next eleven years of school, my thirst for knowledge was never completely quenched. I continued to study and work hard, always striving to prove my ability, maybe in an unconscious effort to still win your approval.

And it worked, didn't it, Mrs. Scarbery? One of the most meaningful aspects of my graduation from high school was the card you mailed to me. Amidst the honors awards, the title of valedictorian, and the other accolades I received at that time, one thing remains a vivid memory—those four little words written by you on that nondescript card:

"I'm proud of you."

RESPECTFULLY,

Linda Bruno

Ocala, Florida

Linda Bruno is a freelance writer, public speaker, and trainer. She is currently working on a devotional entitled All God's Creatures.

5. You Showed Me the Way

Intelligent as we humans are, there are times in each of our lives when we stray from the path we've set for ourselves. Whether the detour is intentional or random, we often find ourselves questioning all that we do, wondering if the goals we set and the ambitions we serve are meant for us in this lifetime. But fate is a strange bedfellow, and governed by a destiny that we can only glimpse at rare moments in our existence, we are often given cause to stop and reassess our current path.

At those crossroads in life, decision making becomes an evil jester, tormenting us with a mix of sound judgment and radical thought. Humor becomes mired in self-doubt, and we are desperate for guidance. Teachers are with us throughout our lives, and though it's not always apparent, they suffer the same afflictions the rest of us do. Their strength emanates from within, and while they may not always show their well-worn heels, they travel down the same rocky roads the rest of us do. Their treasure trove of kind words, actions, and resources is invaluable to all whom they encounter. They are beacons of light through violent storms, and their safe haven is meant for all who seek refuge.

How to Make a Peanut Butter and Jelly Sandwich

🍎 **BY ALICE BERGER** 🍎

Dear Mr. Handler,

It always amazed me how you weren't just an ordinary eighth-grade English teacher. When a friend dared you to carry a pocketbook for a year, you eagerly took on the challenge. Then our eighth-grade class dared you to pierce your ear, and the next day you were wearing a diamond stud. But it was your unorthodox teaching style that really made an impact on all your students at Mineola Junior High School in New York in 1979.

Your obvious love of words and their clever uses jumped out at us in the signs that covered almost every square inch of the classroom. Every day we stared at such gems as *Eschew Obfuscation*, *Egress* (with an arrow pointing right), and *Old Postmen Don't Die—They Just Lose Their Zip*. Even though I've forgotten most of the unusual sayings on those posters, I'll always remember one unique writing experience you gave us that year.

The assignment seemed innocuous enough. All we had to do was write the directions for making a peanut butter and jelly sandwich. By the age of thirteen, we had made dozens of them, and we thought we were experts at the task. It should have been a simple exercise.

We walked into the room that day, expecting to hand in our papers and wait a few days for our grades, as usual—but you had other ideas. We gathered in a circle around one desk, which had been prearranged for our class. On it sat a jar of peanut butter, a jar of jelly, a loaf of bread, and various flatware pieces. I started to get nervous when I got an inkling of what was about to happen.

Smirking, you picked up one of the pages we turned in and began to read: "Take two pieces of bread." You looked at the loaf, then back at us, and asked, "Don't you think I should open the bag first?" A few kids snickered. You opened the bag, and then broke off the corners of one slice. "There—two pieces of bread." One girl's face turned bright red.

You continued to read. "Spread peanut butter on one piece of bread." You picked up the jar and placed it on top of one of the pieces and asked, "How do I spread it?" We all burst out laughing.

This process continued with all the papers that neglected to mention using any kind of spreading utensil, opening the jars, how much peanut butter or jelly to put on the bread, or even which sides of the bread were stuck together. You ended up a sticky mess, and there were no peanut butter and jelly sandwiches to show for your efforts. Although the experiment failed miserably in producing an edible product, it succeeded in teaching us the value of precision in our writing.

In my various office positions over the past fifteen years, I've often had to write directions on how to perform a variety of repetitive tasks. These pages became parts of procedure manuals for those jobs, and have been followed repeatedly with successful results. Managers now rely on me to write them. Maybe that's because I learned the proper way to explain how to make a peanut butter and jelly sandwich?

FONDLY,

Alice (Sigler) Berger
Gouldsboro, Pennsylvania

Alice Berger is an accountant and lives in the Pocono Mountains with her husband and three cats. She writes as a hobby in her spare time.

The Ring Bearer

🍎 By Donna Surgenor Reames 🍎

Dear Mrs. Storey,

Today is my forty-fifth birthday. I don't know if you will remember this, but I can't forget it, even though it happened thirty years ago.

I was fifteen years old, and my mother and three sisters and I had moved that year from Ohio to Pine Mountain, Georgia. My dad hugged us goodbye and promised to join us as soon as he finished up at his job. That was the last time I would see him for about ten years. You already know this . . . he never came.

Mama worked at a local hotel in the tiny town we lived in. Mama didn't make much money, so I got after-school jobs at a small library and at a downtown store. I didn't work for money for new clothes or makeup or going to the movies. I worked to help pay our bills.

You were my favorite high school teacher. I thought you were beautiful, like Sophia Loren. Your dark eyes always sparkled, and I loved the way you pulled your dark hair away from your face. You taught with a liveliness and spirit that kept us all involved and interested in your classes. I wanted to be like you someday. I hoped and prayed to be like you.

One day our class rings arrived. Mine was the most glorious thing I'd ever seen. Tiger's eye, gold and gleaming, in the tiniest gold ring size. I loved that ring. *HCHS. Class of '78*, the engraving said. I sat in my seat and turned the ring around and around in my hand. The thing was, I didn't have the money to pay for it. Our budget barely stretched far enough for macaroni and cheese for my little sisters and the baked beans Mama cooked because they kept us "filled up." I prayed so hard that afternoon in class that God would somehow send me the money.

When the bell rang, I raced to the school bus and ran all three blocks from the bus stop to my grandfather's house. I found my mother and made her give me my father's new phone number. I dialed with my fingers trembling, but I was certain he would help me. After all, I'd prayed, hadn't I? And my belief in God and in the awesome power of prayer was, I thought, unshakable.

My dad answered on the fourth ring. I told him all about my class ring. How pretty it was, how much I wanted it, how everybody was going to get one.

"Dad," I managed to mention, "the only thing is, I need a twenty-dollar deposit for it, and then I can pay the rest later."

I will never forget the dead silence that lay heavy and dull between us. My heart fell. I couldn't believe it. He wasn't going to help me.

"I'm sorry, honey," he finally answered, slowly and quietly, "but I've just spent all my money on a car. I wish I'd known."

I hung up the phone without saying goodbye. I felt something deeper than the loss of my ring. I felt betrayed by God. I'd prayed so hard. And he hadn't answered me.

The next day I stood by your desk as the bell rang. You saw something in my eyes that concerned you, and you laid one hand on my shoulder as I fought back the tears.

"Donna, what's happened to you?" you asked gently.

"I can't . . . my dad . . . no ring . . . no money . . . I hate him!" I started out slowly and ended with a furious burst. "I hate him so much!"

The next moment you became a life teacher for me, teaching me a lesson I've recalled many times over the last three decades, one I've passed on to my pediatric psych patients and to my own three daughters.

"Donna," you said, staring straight into my eyes, "hating your father isn't hurting him. It's only hurting you. If you continue to hate him, it will destroy you someday. Hating always does that. It destroys things. It destroys people."

The tears came and I sobbed. All the pain, the sadness at losing my father, the hurt at his not helping us, never sending child support, loving another woman and other children, the fear of not having enough money, the embarrassment of wearing hand-me-down clothes in the tenth grade, the resentment at having to work all the time while my friends had fun—it all came pouring out in that one moment in your empty classroom.

You let me cry. You told me, over and over again, that my life was better than this, that I was a winner, that I could make something beautiful out of the pain if I wanted to. Or I could give in to the pain, the hate, and the resentment and I could let it destroy everything good and strong and beautiful in my life.

Mrs. Lou Anne Storey, what you did that day was restore my faith. In God. In other people. But mostly, in myself.

I know somehow you were involved, as someone sponsored me for my class ring. I got it, wore it, and loved it for years till I was in nursing school and I gave it as a religious offering at the First Baptist Church of Atlanta. It always meant so much to me. When I looked at it, I thought of you—of one wonderful teacher who cared enough to do more than teach from a book. A woman who gave from her heart and cared enough to make certain that one young girl didn't succumb to bitterness and doubt.

I've grown up now, Mrs. Storey. I'm a single mom to three gorgeous little girls. I got my nursing degree. I started writing and earned awards and won contests for my essays and stories. And I learned to be a survivor.

When I found out four months ago I had a brain tumor, I knew already it wouldn't do me any good to blame anyone, especially God. I thought of you and wondered what you would say if I told you about my tumor.

"Donna," I imagined you saying, "you can take this hurt and let it destroy you or you can make something beautiful out of the pain."

So I listened, Mrs. Storey, just like I did thirty years ago. I accepted my tumor as a wake-up call, and went on about the business of living my life fully, wholly, and with more passion than ever before.

I can't predict my future. None of us can. But I can applaud my past. And I can applaud you, the most amazing teacher I have ever known.

THANKS AGAIN,

Donna Surgenor Reames
Charleston, South Carolina

Donna Surgenor Reames is a single mom to three amazing daughters: Zoe, Chloe, and Caroline. She works as a pediatric psychiatric nurse at the Medical University of South Carolina and is pursuing her nurse practitioner's license.

Charlotte and Friends

🍎 By Jessica Kropf 🍎

The first time I steped into Mrs. Wampler's room, I felt so happy to be in her class Sometimes Mrs Wampler gets mad, but she was a geat teacher and I will miss her very much. And I liked science we did lots of fun projects, we studied about rocks that were made from lava like obsidian, basalt, pumice, quartz, and granite.

For five weeks my class got to study the Rainforest. it was fun i got to learn about a lot of animals like the ocelot. I also learned that everyday 5000 trees get cut down and there is only 7 rainforests left in the world. I loved Charlotte's web it was so fun. Charlotte had 540 eggs and Wilbur had Charlotte as a best friend and Wilbur was sad when Charlotte died. And I just had the best time ever it was fun and i learned alot.

thank you Mrs. Wampler for being my teacher. thank you for everything.

Jessica Kropf

Toledo, Oregon

Jessica Kropf is a ten-and-a-half-year-old fifth grader who loves to swim and do art.

Opportunity Knocks

🍎 By Dera R. Williams 🍎

Dear Mrs. Jackson,

The saying "hindsight is 20/20" is not a cliché, but an actual fact. When you were my eighth-grade homemaking teacher, I didn't appreciate your attention to detail. When you insisted on the exact measurements for cooking, I found it annoying. The stern warning that the stitches had to be straight and even on the zipper of the A-line skirt I was sewing felt stifling. The admonition of the importance of keeping a budget went in one ear and out the other.

You were unwavering in drilling the right way to perform tasks, and adamant that my classmates and I complete assignments and do them well. Why were these things so important? Why did we need to learn this stuff anyway?

It seemed you were more rigid with us African-American girls (we were Negro back then), and sometimes we resented it. It was 1963, at Alexander Hamilton Junior High School in Oakland, California. We were the generation of young girls of middle-class, upwardly mobile black families of the 1960s who had lived the struggle in the southern states, wanted a better life for their families, and migrated to California to avail themselves of the opportunities that this state had to offer. We skinny-legged brown and tan-skinned girls with our straggly ponytails could not see beyond our self-centered needs of living for the moment. Boys, dancing to the music of Stevie Wonder, and trying to keep up with current dress styles were our main focus.

We were so silly.

We California-bred girls used to laugh at your southern mannerisms and mocked your Texas accent behind your back. But you were proud as you stood before the class, your horn-rimmed glasses sitting on your nose, your head erect, and wisps of curly black hair escaping from the tightly wrapped bun on the back of your head.

We just took it all for granted—our neighborhoods, our classmates, and our studies were there for the taking. Without a doubt, we were going places. How could we know then how significant those skills you drilled into us would be in the future? That they are just as important, or more so, as managing a corporation, administering a hospital budget, raising funds for nonprofit organizations, or starting a business?

These opportunities are available to us, but they were not available for you as a young woman in the segregated South during the '40s and '50s. We didn't know what you had to go through to obtain your education and the limitations placed on you, even with a college degree.

But then we grew up, and fortunately those nagging annoyances you insisted upon became lifesavers. Because you took pride in what you taught, we were able to take those skills and come to the realization of how important they are. Homemaking skills got us through college and young adulthood, and then motherhood. Learning the simple things taught us how to slow down.

There were times, as I was sewing a hem in my daughter's dress, that I paused to reflect. I thought of the pride I'd felt when I'd completed my A-line skirt and modeled it in our fashion show.

On the nights when corporate America becomes too much, we baby boomers can immerse ourselves in the pride of small accomplishments. We can pass on to our daughters the importance of being well-rounded young women—that they too can bring home the bacon and cook it many different ways.

THANK YOU, MRS. JACKSON.

Dera Jones Williams
Oakland, California

Dera R. Williams lives, works, and plays in Oakland, California, the setting of many childhood memories that are being compiled into a volume of short stories. Her memoir pieces have appeared in A Cup of Comfort for Women *and* Peralta Press: A West Coast Journal.

A Picture Tells a Thousand Tales

By Louise Weller Craven

Dear Dr. Barbara Johnson,

You won't remember me, but I was in your Children's
Literature class at Chico State College in 1973, a
student in the Elementary Teacher Credential Program.
I discovered that you and I share a love of picture
books, and my love for them was rekindled when I
enrolled in your class.

After receiving a B.A. in Humanities from Chico
State, I had to decide what to do for a living. In the
1960s and early 1970s, girls had three choices: you
could be a secretary, a nurse, or a teacher. I knew I
didn't want to be a secretary or nurse, so I began the
course work to become a teacher. I floundered for a
semester, unsure and uncommitted until my first day
in your class. In you I saw a pleasant young woman
with a calm, intelligent demeanor who had built a
career around a subject she loved—reading. I thought,
Okay, I can do this. I can be a teacher.

It was during your class that I recalled my early
childhood memories and weekly trips to the library
with my father. I was five or six years old when
these trips began, and my father would leave me in
the children's section as he searched the grown-ups'
shelves. I'd sit at a little table with a pile of well-worn
picture books, their oily covers frayed at the corners,

exposing little strings that you could pull ever so slowly until they snapped. Dr. Seuss was my favorite author.

One evening upon our return home, my mother complained to my father, "Louise should be reading literature, not picture books." So on our next trip to the library, I checked out *Wind in the Willows,* but I never got around to reading it. By the time I was nine, I had stopped reading for fun because we'd bought a television. How I missed those picture books!

Imagine how thrilled I was when your first class assignment was for us to go to the local library and read picture books. Oh boy! I met *The Snowy Day, Where the Wild Things Are, Blueberries for Sal, Make Way for Ducklings,* and *Caps for Sale,* and my old friend Ferdinand the bull. Like me, Ferdinand preferred wildflowers and daydreams to fighting in the competitive arena.

When you introduced us to the Caldecott and Newbery Award winners, I dreamt of winning a medal. I don't have a medal yet, but it's not out of the question. After several decades of teaching children and adults, I've retired. Every now and then, an advertisement arrives in the mail for a correspondence course in writing for children, and I'm tempted to sign up. Should I try to write for a living? What did you do after you retired?

Thank you, Dr. Johnson, for reintroducing me to children's literature and for understanding that we're never too old to enjoy picture books.

SINCERELY,

Louise Weller Craven
Davis, California

Louise Weller Craven is a credentialed elementary and ESL instructor. She enjoys traveling to and writing about the CBS Survivor *filming locations. Her photos and articles have been published on numerous Internet Web sites and are quoted in university textbooks.*

Looking Beyond the Norm

🍎 BY RICHARD CROWHURST 🍎

Dear Mrs. Smith,

This letter is a bit different from the normal ones I've sent you with updates about the family and the dog's latest scrapes. What I haven't told you before, because I couldn't quite find the words, is just how important you and your teachings are to me. It's probably because of you that I've ended up doing something I could have only dreamed of—even if it isn't what either of us would have predicted thirteen years ago.

I was fifteen when I first became one of your students at Oakwood Park Grammar School in Maidstone, Kent. How can I explain your importance to me back then? There isn't just one, self-contained anecdote that sums up what, or how, you taught me. It was a slow process over four or five years, like the osmosis you taught in your biology classes.

During those years, you taught me far more than the details of photosynthesis and the nitrogen cycle. In your lessons, we covered much more than the rigors of scientific method. We covered life, and how to live it.

The most important things you taught me were to believe what I discovered for myself and not just to rely on what I was told by other people. Most importantly, you taught me to believe in my own abilities and to have faith in what I could achieve with hard work and dedication.

The ability to distract you with a huge range of vaguely philosophical topics was one of the things that made all of us love your biology lessons. Do you remember how we'd all escape to your room at break times to catch up on our work? It was your benevolent approach to teaching us that made you seem even more special.

You supported me in a number of ways. From the first morning I returned to school after my mother had died, when you comforted and encouraged me, to that evening in the youth hostel, when a few of us declined the attractions of the local pub to stay up and discuss philosophy, politics, and the natural world with you.

There were some classic moments in your lessons over the course of three years. Many of them still bring a smile to my lips when I remember them: Roy bringing in a dead, flea-infested fox for dissection; the immortal locusts for dissection that just wouldn't die (how many methods of execution did you try in the end?); getting told on for playing with pigs' eyeballs and for leaving the school greenhouse infested with whiteflies after my final year exam project. Much of my time at school was far more miserable than I let on to anyone at the time, but I always looked forward to your lessons and your wisdom.

I'm grateful that we've kept in touch over all these years. It doesn't seem possible, when I read your letters at Christmas, filled with the activities of your children, that I remember you taking maternity leave for the first time. Then again, as I sit here with the memories of fifteen years ago flooding back, it seems hard to believe that I'm married now, with a wonderful little girl of my own. I just hope that as she grows up, she finds someone who inspires her as much as you inspired me.

I suppose what I'm trying to say, in a rather longwinded way, is that there isn't just one single lesson that you taught me. You nurtured and nudged me just enough to release my potential, which is exactly what a great teacher should do. Before I even entered college, you taught me that the most important things I would engage in were the late-night discussions and the long-term friendships I would make. You also taught me that two words are better than four, and that it was possible to respect—even to love—someone with a different outlook on life than my own. You took the raw material you were presented with and turned it into someone who, I hope, has turned out all right.

Thanks again for everything, Mrs. Smith. As usual, I'm looking forward to hearing all your news this Christmas. Maybe next year we'll be able to get together like we keep promising.

YOURS,

Richard

Lincolnshire, England

Richard Crowhurst is a freelance writer and author based in Lincolnshire, eastern England, where he lives with his family and their pets. He specializes in writing about history and farming topics. www.freelance-writer-and-author.co.uk

Teaching Mother and Son
🍎 BY LUCY ARMSTRONG 🍎

Dear Miss Lyke,

You were my son Johnny's second-grade teacher in
Kingston, New York, but during that time you taught
me as well. Johnny was an energetic, inquisitive, and
often impulsive kid. It was the early '70s, and though
he was only seven years old, I already worried that his
inability to sit still in school would get him into trouble
later in life, as it already had in the first grade. But you
encouraged Johnny (and his equally energetic friend
Paul) to explore life fully while channeling his energy to
meet society's norms when absolutely necessary.

Your example showed me that Johnny could be
both energetic and socially appropriate when the
situation demanded it. From you I learned to accept
my son in an unconditional way. After Johnny had you
for a teacher, my goal was to encourage him to channel
his energy instead of suppressing it. You were Johnny's
teacher, but you taught both of us.

A favorite family story is how Johnny and his
friend Paul caught bees in plastic bags (that were
meant to hold lunch sandwiches) and then brought the
bees into your classroom. You turned it into a lesson on
bees for the entire class. After a short discussion on the
anatomy of bees (including their ability to sting), you
told the boys to take the bees outside and turn them

loose. When asked recently, Johnny said, "I never even got stung."

You taught me that by giving Johnny more freedom, I would be gaining more control as a mother. It's okay to hop, skip, jump, run, and dance on the sidewalk on the way to school, but when it's time to cross the street, there is a need to walk carefully and watch for cars. There's a time to let energy loose and there's a time to focus.

I watched John successfully alternate his pattern of "energy releasing" and "focusing" as he grew up. He married a woman who, like you, could appreciate both sides of his nature. She accepts the motorcycle rides to Sturgis, the dune buggy, the truck with the huge wheels, and John's stories of close calls. John has worked for the Mayo Clinic for almost twenty-five years, so he's also shown his steady, responsible side.

John's twin girls are the same age as John was when he had you for a teacher. I see him encouraging the girls' adventurous side by getting them a trampoline and putting up a twenty-five-foot rope ladder on the tree in the backyard. Both girls are also expected to respect adults and do well in school. The girls like to hear stories about when dad was their age, and the name Miss Lyke comes up every time. John recognizes what a gift you gave him in the second grade, and he wants to pass it on to his children.

I remember that years later you told me that you were also an inquisitive, impulsive, energetic child who often felt repressed. As a teacher, you wanted to encourage similar children to meet both their own needs and the needs of society. I feel that you succeeded with John. At the same time you taught me to see the advantage in his energy. Thank you for seeing the best in my son and for teaching us both how to enjoy his enthusiasm for life.

GRATEFULLY YOURS,

Lucy
Rochester, Minnesota

Lucy Armstrong is a recently retired nurse with four grown children, six grandchildren, and one great-grandchild. She recently started freelance writing and hopes to be the Grandma Moses of literature.

What You Didn't Know
🍎 BY BROOKE BERGAN 🍎

Dear Ms. Kormeier,

I had you as my third-grade music teacher in Waynesville, Missouri, in 1991. You auditioned me and placed me in your honor choir, but your impact on my life goes far beyond music. There was much you didn't know.

Throughout my childhood I endured many types of abuse, some from my mom, who also taught music, and some from a teenage boy who'd abused me sexually the year before I met you. I wanted so much to talk about these things, but I feared you wouldn't understand. After all, you and my mom were friends, though at times I wondered if maybe you'd befriended her just so she'd let you be friends with me.

Once you volunteered to babysit my brother and I, and you spent time helping me with my spelling before bed. Another time you took me to McDonald's on a snowy day and let me pick out anything I wanted, then paid for it with your own money. I was a sensitive child, and your actions had a bigger impact than you could've imagined.

There was one particular incident that proved to be a lesson in trust, and that was a day you were serving as lunchroom monitor. The other kids at my table were especially noisy that day and refused to quiet down. I sat silently, praying and watching you closely. Finally, you sentenced the entire table—including me—to fifteen minutes on the wall at recess. I couldn't understand why you chose to punish me when you knew I hadn't done anything wrong!

After that incident, I viewed you as a traitor, and had soon plotted ways to convey my bitterness. I slouched in choir—something I knew you'd notice. At times I even refused to sing, focusing instead on nailing you to the blackboard with my angry eight-year-old glare. After a few days of this, you had me stay after class to talk. I thought for sure you'd be mad, but instead of anger I heard love and concern in your voice. Nevertheless, I was stubborn and refused to answer, instead shrugging angrily in response to your questions. That night, sleep evaded me as I struggled to overcome my guilty conscience.

The next day was a cold one. At recess I apologized to you for causing problems. I didn't have my jacket with me, and as evidence I'd been forgiven, you wrapped me in your coat and escorted me back into the building where I could stay warm.

There are other stories, but all have the same theme—a teacher who cared enough to go the extra mile. Because of that I will never forget you, Ms. Kormeier, nor can I forget the impact a few kind words had on one hurting soul. For that, I want to say thank you.

YOUR STUDENT,

Brooke Bergan
Ottumwa, Iowa

Brooke Bergan is a Christian writer from Iowa. She enjoys writing in multiple genres, including fiction, nonfiction, and poetry.

Keeping the Faith

By Jessica McCurdy-Crooks

Dear Mrs. Brown,

How can I ever thank you for all you've done for me? There are so many memories of all the kind words and encouragement you gave me throughout my high school life. That's over twenty years ago since you were my teacher at St. Catherine High School in Spanish Town, but those memories remain as fresh in my mind as if it were yesterday.

I sincerely believe that you're the first "true" Christian I've ever met. Not only do you profess Christ, you live your life as Christ would live his. I have molded my own life after your example, and every time I have to make a choice, I wonder what Christ would have done.

I'll bet you don't remember how you helped me as a twelve-year-old to understand how it is that there are so many different people in the world, yet we were made in God's image. Unlike my pastor, who thought I was being sinful for questioning God's words, you explained it to me as you understood it. You told me that the physical being wasn't the image of God, it was the soul, and it was from then that I started to love you as my mentor. Over the years that love grew until you became my second mother. Ungrateful child that I am, I allowed life and growing up to break the bond between us, but I have always carried you in my heart.

"Jessica, you're a sheep."

Sometimes I find myself wondering if I'm the only one who recalls these words. I was taunted with those words frequently by my fellow classmates on quite a few occasions—some teasingly, others with intent to hurt. But it was just a reminder of the faith you had in me.

One day when I was in grade eleven, you reprimanded the class, stating that some people were sheep and others were goats. Of course, everyone said that I was your pet, and therefore a sheep. That's one of the memories that has stuck with me. Ever since then I've tried to live my life like a sheep—humbly and peacefully.

Even now, Mrs. Brown, with everything I do, I wonder if you would approve. I became a librarian because I wanted to help others the way you helped me. Do you remember lending me an encyclopedia volume to take home? It was our secret, but what an honor that was to me. Over the years, I've treated my students with the same kind of love and respect with which you treated me. I've remained close to some over the years, and I owe it all to you.

I must confess there were a few times when I went against the rules trying to fit in at school, but I promise, it was rare. I stopped the day you came into class and checked for nail polish. You never even looked at me because you had such faith in me to do the right thing. I was so ashamed that I never wore nail polish to school again. And I also swallowed quite a few pieces of gum when I saw you coming!

Most of all I'm thankful for your helping me with lunch money while ensuring that my pride remained intact. Even at the young age of thirteen I saw through your tactics when you would say, "Jessica, can you buy my lunch for me? And just buy something for yourself." After the second time, I understood, but it made me feel good that you didn't offer me charity. Soon you offered me the job of "library prefect," but I knew it was your way of helping me financially. It also helped my self-esteem and confidence, and it meant the world to me to gain your trust.

Being called teacher's pet was a badge of honor. You've molded me into the woman I am today, for which I'm forever grateful. In my heart you'll always be my second mother. I trust it's not too late to return to the fold, the ever-loving prodigal daughter.

YOURS LOVINGLY,

Jessica McCurdy (Crooks)
Old Harbour, St. Catherine, Jamaica

Jessica McCurdy-Crooks is a freelance writer, researcher, editor, and information consultant/librarian. She lives with the love of her life, husband Owen; her son Jalen; and two dogs.

Yin and Yang

By Candy Killion

Dear Mrs. M.,

If you remember me, it may likely amuse you that I'm addressing you formally, and with respect. It's been more than thirty years since we've spoken, and the last time we did I called you Maureen. That was with your permission. But being that it was the early '70s in Newark, New Jersey, and being young and glib and brash, I'd already given myself that license anyway.

More than anything, I wanted to be a writer. That, and, admittedly, class clown. My other high school teachers assigned me either a seat at the back of the room so I wouldn't distract them or a place in the front row so a careful eye could be kept on me.

Looking back, it seems that where I sat is related to how interested I was in the subject at hand. The math and science teachers kept a close watch on my shiftless boredom, but in English literature, the seat at the back of the class was fine. I was alert and loud during discussions of *Beowulf,* so being in the back was just a little easier on everyone's ears.

During that era the times were changing, and where they changed most for me was in your class, where a seat was earned. I learned what I needed to know in other places, sometimes with enthusiasm and often with reluctance. But you caught my attention—by not giving me any. You taught sociology to the upperclassmen, and moderated the school newspaper. The first time I walked into the newsroom meeting, loaded with an armory of sarcastic comments and a bloated ego because I was the only freshman in the place, you looked over your horn-rimmed glasses at me and said, "So you think you're that good? Prove it."

Over the next couple of years I was still not officially in any of your classes. I turned in perfect copy, and you'd blue-pencil it and send it flying back at me. I couldn't understand. My essays wowed the English class (at least those who didn't fall asleep). But you would grunt, cock your head, and say, "Cut the crap out."

When my senior year rolled around, I knew I wanted to be in your sociology class. Still armed with cockiness, I figured it was the least I could do in the way of revenge. My place in the newspaper hung by a string most weeks, but you kept me on my toes. I wanted to keep you on yours.

"Where do I sit?" I said, walking into your classroom.

I waited for a groan from you—anything of shock value.

Instead, you waved me to the back. "If it turns out you have anything constructive to say, you may make it to the front."

Against my will, I did not sleep, eat, or gaze aimlessly out the window when I was in your class. There was too much going on, as most days you tossed the textbook aside in favor of more topical conversation.

"Want to assess modern culture? Watch commercials tonight. What do they tell you? Want to be able to read higher than eighth-grade level? From now on, you will subscribe to the Sunday *New York Times*."

I cracked jokes, and you threw out challenges. By the time we'd both survived my final year in high school, you wrote in my yearbook,

"In spite of all the insults and agony you've put me through, I've enjoyed having you to kick around."

—Maureen

Back of the class, front of the class, by then it didn't really matter. You kicked me there, you kicked me here. You met me word for word and forced me to stretch in a way that no other teacher had. You taught me to think outside the box, to question, to argue my stand, and to never settle for the mediocre.

I walked into your class with revenge in mind, but three decades later, I bow to you, Mrs. "M." Revenge is yours, and it is a dish best served straight up.

THANK YOU,

Candy Killion
Davie, Florida

Candy Killion is a freelance writer who has contributed to Adams Media's Rocking Chair Reader *and* Cup of Comfort *series and* Chicken Soup for the Healthy Living Soul: Menopause. *She is also the recipient of the 2005 Chistell Prize for poetry.*

Sunny

🍎 BY PARISE ZELENY 🍎

Dear Sunny,

Thank you for hunting for bugs and insects, because I like to see a ladybug. I like that you are so nice to me. I like to play with the castle, and I like to play with the king and queen. You're my favorite teacher because I like the way you talk—beautiful.

Sunny is special because I want to tell her that I like fairies.

LOVE,

PARISE

Monterey Peninsula, California

Parise Zeleny is a three-year-old preschooler who loves to dictate letters to friends, family, and teachers—as long as someone is willing to listen and transcribe. Once she can write for herself, there will be no stopping her, and the world will be flooded with missives.

Almost Heaven

🍎 By Lynn R. Hartz, Ph.D. 🍎

Dear Dr. Christopherson,

You may not remember, but I absolutely hated where I grew up and lived. I grew up in a "holler" in West Virginia, and did not like being considered a hillbilly. My previous work experiences had taken me all over the United States, but I still felt the sting of being teased about being from West Virginia. I wanted only to escape my roots and move elsewhere—anywhere—I didn't think it would matter where.

But I was wrong, and my time with you in Arizona proved that.

In your wisdom, every time we had a writing assignment, you insisted I write about what I knew, which was my Appalachian heritage and my family roots. As such, I did research on Appalachian culture, only to find out that I already knew everything that was written. It was as though I could have written the research from observations of my own family and my own life.

So, I wrote about West Virginia, with a focus on family life. I explained their religion, how people name their children, how families communicate and relate to each other, and how truly related the communities are in Appalachia. As I wrote about my roots and observed others from various cultures, through the school, the community, or those stationed in Tucson with the military, I began to appreciate my heritage.

My daughter was born while I was attending school there, and yes, she was named after my father and my mother, a strong Appalachian trait honoring the family members for whom the name is given. My father was so pleased to have a granddaughter named after him!

My husband died nineteen months after my baby was born. The Air Force had sent personnel to inform me of my husband's death. I was devastated beyond belief, and was expecting our second child. I called your office and left a message for you. Your concern and kindness were overwhelming to me then, even as they are now. As soon as you received the message, you came to my house. No, I certainly was not okay. You knew that immediately and put your arms around me while I sobbed until I thought I had no tears left.

That was not the usual thing for a professor to do for a student, but it most definitely was the right thing. Your care and concern went beyond the classroom to the very heart of this student.

After I returned from burying my husband at home in West Virginia, you asked me what I was planning to do. "I'm going home," I said. Home to West Virginia, to my family and my roots. As I left Arizona, John Denver's *Country Roads* brought me all the way home and helped me love and appreciate the beauty of where I live.

I learned so much from you, Dr. Christopherson, but the most important thing I learned was that I am a "hillbilly gal." I love my West Virginian Appalachian roots and family. I love my mountains. I managed to finish a Ph.D. and serve on government committees related to Appalachian and rural women.

May you know that not only did you touch my life as a student, but you changed my life as a woman and a professional. I did a nontraditional Ph.D. and dedicated my dissertation to you. My doctorate specifies that my degree is "psychotherapy with an emphasis on women and Appalachian culture. . ."

I only hope that others recognize you for being the professor you are, and a person who has affected so many. You knew me as perhaps no one else ever has or ever will, and I will always be grateful that your influence sent me home to *"almost heaven."*

BEST WISHES,

Lynn R. Hartz, Ph.D.
Charleston, West Virginia

Dr. Lynn R. Hartz, a former psychotherapist, is the author of Club Fed, Living Inside a Women's Prison, And Time Stood Still, *and* Praise Him in Prison, *and has contributed to several anthologies, including the* Cup of Comfort *and* Rocking Chair *series.*

Nothing Is What It Seems to Be

🍎 By Izaddin Syah Yusof 🍎

My Dear Miss Lee,

Do you remember our first class together in 1992 at Muar High School in Johor?

There we sat, a group of sixteen-year-olds who were learning English as a second language. You entered the class, introduced yourself, and started telling our class that English is one of the most difficult languages to master. You then went on to the topic of pronunciation, and mentioned that when it comes to English pronunciation, not everything sounds like we think it should sound. "Nothing is what it seems to be in the English language."

Without delay, you turned to the blackboard and scribbled out a single word: *Arkansas*

"How does one pronounce the name of this American state?" you asked in your most officious tone.

"Ar-kehn-saw," I said, with perfect pronunciation.

All eyes turned to me.

As if in slow motion, you turned around and issued a steely glare as if I'd just given away the fact that Darth Vader was Luke Skywalker's father.

I can't remember what I did next. The classroom was so quiet. Did I hide under the table or laugh out loud? Or did I do both?

Without giving any indication as to whether my answer was correct, you turned your back to us and wrote another word on the board: *Tucson*

For what seemed like an eternity, the room was still. *Why isn't anybody saying anything? Are they afraid Miss Lee's patented Glare of Death will obliterate them?* My initial impulse was to stay quiet, but just as you were about to crack a little victory smirk, my lips let loose.

"Too-sawn," I said, knowing full well the pronunciation was correct.

Now I'm no mind reader, but I could've sworn a few choice expletives were swirling in your head. *Things are gonna get good around here,* I thought.

And so they did.

That was only the beginning of a not-so-subtle two-year game of cat and mouse.

I have to concede that I was so convinced that you had something personal against me that I practically sabotaged most of my class work. I remember the time when we had to write an essay on the ethics of journalism. Plagiarism became my friend as I lifted entire paragraphs from a library book. Plagiarism on the ethics of journalism—how sweet the irony! (I admit what I did was wrong, but in hindsight I realize that it was a test to see if you were paying attention.)

By the next class, you proved you were still a step ahead of me. You began by mentioning that one of the essays was the work of a genuine author—and you didn't mean that in a good way. You then quoted the name of the publication the text was swiped from. *Aha! My evil plot had worked!*

Or so I thought . . .

I still can't fathom why you didn't call me out in front of the whole class. I guess the thought that you actually had a heart didn't spring to mind. Instead, you spent the entire class discussing plagiarism, your fiery eyes set upon me as you spoke. Lost in my victory, I stared coolly off into oblivion, not realizing that I may have proved a point—but not well enough. After all, you did go to the extent of finding the exact book I copied from!

Our little game played on until I left for college. Sometimes I would win, and sometimes you would win. We parted without saying goodbye, and without me saying thank you for being my teacher.

Miss Lee, you may not be my favorite teacher, but you certainly left an impact on my life without my realizing it until many years later. In hindsight, I was a naive student, and you had only my best interest at heart. You are special to me because out of all the teachers I've had you are the one who constantly comes to mind.

And you were right, Miss Lee. In regard to your teaching, and the English language—nothing is what it seems to be.

Sincerely,

Izaddin Syah Yusof
Petaling Jaya, Malaysia

Izaddin Syah Yusof is a Kuala Lumpur–based yuppie. Never in a million years did he think his teacher would be an inspiration for a short story, but then again, nothing is what it seems to be.

Discipline Master

🍎 By Nesta Primeau 🍎

Dear Mr. Whitley,

You were my high school principal in 1960 at John Oliver High School in Vancouver, BC. I was one of those students whose presence was hardly ever required in your office. In fact, I had visited you only once before throughout my high school years—to receive an award I'd won in an essay contest.

But, my dear principal, I didn't keep all school rules—at least not all the time. The last occasion you and I met in your office was for a matter of discipline. Your academics-focused, rule-abiding student had played hooky. I covered my unauthorized absence with a note that began,

"Please excuse Nesta . . . headache . . . heavy cold . . ."

It was an ominous list of symptoms for an afternoon's absence on a warm day in May. It ended with an approximation of my mother's signature.

Several days passed before the consequences of playing hooky unfolded.

"Nesta," said my mother, "there was a phone call from Mr. Whitley. Were you absent from school on Tuesday?"

I admitted my guilt. Mother wept and wailed. She was not used to dealing with a wayward daughter.

"I lied for you," she sobbed. My heart leapt with hope. Could it be that my mother had discerned I played hooky and forged a note? Could it be that she supported my claim of illness when you called?

Mother had discerned no such thing. She told you that I had been in school. My deception was obvious.

I anticipated facing you and I was terrified. Would you assign detention? I'd never served an official school detention and dreaded the possibility of blemishing my school record. Would you scold me? Could I be suspended?

A week passed before you left a message with my homeroom teacher—my presence was requested in your office.

It wasn't easy for my legs to carry me down the stairs, down the hallway, and into the valley of the shadow of death. The main exit was tempting, and I nearly bolted.

You stood in the office foyer surrounded by three women. For a moment I wondered if my crime was so severe that you had summoned school board representatives—but these people were not from our city. I was introduced.

"They teach school in Australia," you said. "Show them around our building, please."

The walk to your office was my punishment, and it *was* effective.

YOURS ACROSS THE YEARS,

Nesta Primeau, *née Owen*
Surrey, British Columbia, Canada

For the past fifteen years, Nesta Primeau has operated a small business writing resumes. Interacting with clients gives meaning to her days.